Why Jesus?

S.Masood

Why follow Jesus?

OM
publishing

First published in the UK 1997 by OM Publishing

03 02 01 00 99 98 97   7 6 5 4 3 2 1

OM Publishing is an imprint of Patemoster Publishing,
P.O. Box 300, Carlisle, Cumbria, CA3 0QS U.K.

Unless otherwise indicated, all Qur'anic references are taken from
The Meaning of the Glorious Qur'an, tr. Marmaduke Pickthal.
Published in Pakistan by Taj Company Ltd.

British Library Cataloguing in Publication Data

A catalogue record for this book is available from the British Library

ISBN 1-85078-264-4

Typeset by WestKey Ltd., Falmouth, Cornwall
Printed in the UK by Mackays of Chatham PLC, Kent

Contents

Contents

Introduction

Both Islam and Christianity share the belief that God appointed prophets and apostles to lead humanity into the straight path. God inspired and sent his revelation to such people for guidance. Today that revelation is available to us in printed form.

Muslims and Christians are familiar with names like Adam, Abraham, Isaac, Jacob, Moses, David, Solomon and Jesus. While Islam and Christianity share the belief in Jesus as the Word and the Spirit of God, Christianity takes a few but crucial steps further. It claims Jesus as the Saviour of humanity, sent by God for this purpose.

People are more quizzical about things around than ever before. They question Why and How. Their inquiry questions the Christian faith too. We do realize that not everyone, including most Muslims, has the time or energy to read long books. For this reason an abridged version of a response to such an interest, who

Jesus was and why follow him, is presented in the following pages.

Answers to who Jesus is and to why follow him are given into a down-to-earth perspective to make it suitable and readable for those to whom English may be a second language. Though honorific titles are not printed along with every name, the author and the publisher hold the names of the prophets and apostles in highest respect.

Chapter 1

The Book

For Muslims the Qur'an and the Ahadith (traditions) are the foremost authority. For Christians it is the Bible, which is a resource centre of the Christian faith. It is a collection or library of books. The word 'Bible' itself comes from the Greek word '*biblia*', which means 'the books'.

The 66 books in the Bible were written down by a number of God's people over a period of 1,500 years in three languages. They were from many walks of life: they were prophets, kings, shepherds, fishermen, scholars, a soldier, a civil servant, a doctor, and missionaries. Although these people were from different walks of life and lived at different times, all were called by God for one purpose: to proclaim his word.

There are many books beside the Bible that tell us great truths, but the Bible is different. It tells us not only about the existence of a holy God, who created us all and loves us, but also, that we have lost our way to him because of sin. It tells us how we can get back to him and be in his presence forever.

The contents of the Bible

The Bible is divided into two sections, the Old Testament and the New Testament. These focus on the two great relationships called 'covenants' that God made: the first with the nation of Israel, through Moses, and the second with all humanity, through Jesus.

The Old Testament

The Old Testament records God's dealings with the people of Israel on the basis of the covenant he made with them through Moses. The earlier part tells of the creation of man, the Flood, the call of Abraham, and the setting apart of the people of Israel through the line of Isaac and Jacob.

After the miraculous deliverance of the people of Israel from slavery in Egypt, and the establishment of the covenant and the law through Moses, the Old Testament records the history of God's relationship with Israel. It also tells us about the ups and downs of this nation, their rebellion against God, the many prophetic warnings and the punishment that God brought on Israel. Along with this we also find a line of prophecies concerning a coming Saviour, the Messiah, and the giving of a new covenant.

The New Testament

The New Testament is the story of the fulfilment of these prophecies and the new covenant that God made through Jesus, known to Muslim friends through the Qur'an as *Al-Masih*, *Isa*, or *Ibn Maryam*. The message of the New Testament centres around the holiness of God and his provision, through Jesus Christ, of salvation for mankind. The gospel introduces the Saviour to us. The chapters of Acts describe the spread of the gospel, the good news about salvation. The letters give details of the blessings of that salvation, while the last book, called Revelation, previews the climax of salvation.

However, some may ask, 'All this was written long ago. How has the Bible come down to us? Is this Bible essentially the same as it was when it left those earlier hands? Are we sure that none of the original has been lost? Has anything been added to the Bible which ought not to be there?' In the later chapters we will deal with these and other questions in the light of the evidence available to us.

The order of the books of the Bible

The arrangement of the books does not follow the order in which they were written down, although the first book, Genesis, records the earliest times, and Revelation, the last book, tells of the end times. However, the books are arranged according to their literary type or style. In the Old Testament, the first five books are known as 'the books of the law'; Joshua to Esther are 'the historical books'; Job to the Song of Songs are known as 'the writings' or sometimes, as 'the wisdom writings', and Isaiah to Malachi are 'the prophetic books'. In the New Testament, the first four books are biographical accounts of Jesus' life; Acts is a historical account of the early church. Romans to Jude are letters, and Revelation is written in language known as 'apocalyptic'.

A list of the 39 Old Testament books and 27 New Testament books can be found in the contents page towards the front of any Bible.

The Names and Order of the Books of the Bible

The Old Testament

Genesis	1 Kings	Ecclesiastes	Obadiah
Exodus	2 Kings	Song of Songs	Jonah
Leviticus	1 Chronicles	Isaiah	Micah
Numbers	2 Chronicles	Jeremiah	Nahum
Deuteronomy	Ezra	Lamentations	Habakkuk
Joshua	Nehemiah	Ezekiel	Zephaniah
Judges	Esther	Daniel	Haggai
Ruth	Job	Hosea	Zechariah
1 Samuel	Psalms	Joel	Malachi
2 Samuel	Proverbs	Amos	

The New Testament

The Gospel	Galatians	Hebrews
According to Matthew	Ephesians	James
According to Mark	Colossians	1 Peter
According to Luke	1 Thessalonians	2 Peter
According to John	2 Thessalonians	1 John
Acts of the Apostles	1 Timothy	2 John
Romans	2 Timothy	3 John
1 Corinthians	Titus	Jude
2 Corinthians	Philemon	Revelation

Chapter 2

The Bible and the Qur'an

It is interesting to know that the Qur'an also upholds the Bible as the word of God. It is God who revealed the Scriptures. The usual term in the Qur'an for the previous scriptures is *'al-kitab'* (the book), and Jews and Christians are identified as *'Ahlul Kitab'* (people of the book). The following terms are also used with reference to parts of the Bible:

1. *Tawrat* – Torah, the first five books of the Bible
2. *Zabur* – the Psalms
3. *Sahaif-e-anbia* – the books of the prophets
4. *Injil* – the Gospel, the New Testament

Both in Islamic and Christian terminology, the word *'Torah'* generally refers to the revelation given to Moses. However, it is also used to describe the sum total of Jewish scriptures, collectively known by Christians as the Old Testament. Similarly, the 'Injil' is used to refer to the whole collection of Holy

Scriptures which Christians call the New Testament.

The Qur'an emphasizes that the Tawrat, the Zabur, the Sahaif and the Injil are all God's books, his word, his light, and '*Furqan*' (criterion). In other words, they are the basis of God's judgement of men.[1]

The universality of the Torah and the Injil is endorsed by the Qur'an and it insists that the Injil and the Torah are guidance for every one, 'clear testimonies for mankind, and a guidance and a mercy'.[2]

Injil as a standard

Christians are told to judge according to the Injil, 'Let the People of the Gospel judge by that which Allah hath revealed therein. Whoso judgeth not by that which Allah hath revealed, such are evil-livers.'[3]

Would the Qur'an have commanded Christians to judge by the Injil if there had been any reason to believe that it was not authentic in every detail?

God's word never changes

The Qur'an claims that no one can alter the word of God, 'It is the law of Allah which hath taken course aforetime. Thou wilt not find for the law of Allah aught of power to change.'[4] Long before the Qur'an, the Bible claimed in similar words, 'The grass withers and the flowers fall, but the word of our God stands for ever.'[5]

The Qur'an does not suggest alteration

In the Qur'an there is no suggestion that the biblical

text has been altered or corrupted. The word *'tahrif'* is never used with reference to the Bible itself. The Qur'an occasionally accuses the Jews of concealing the truth but it never levels this accusation at Christians. It in no way implies that the text of the Bible has been corrupted.

Before Muhammad

Some claim that the Injil and the Torah were corrupted before the rise of Islam. If that were so, why does the Qur'an affirm that the message of Islam was simply a confirmation of the previous Scriptures? According to the Qur'an, which was written approximately six hundred years after the writing of the Injil, the Torah and the Injil were in pure form in Muhammad's time. Had the Injil not been genuine and totally accurate in the time of Muhammad, then the Qur'an ought not to have instructed Christians to judge by that which God had revealed in the Gospel.

After Muhammad

Others maintain that the Torah and the Injil were changed sometime after Muhammad began preaching. However, this charge contradicts the Qur'an's claim to be the guardian of the previous inspired books.[6] Thus, anyone who asserts that there has been corruption of the text of the Torah or of the Injil also, inevitably, charges the Qur'an with failure in its role as guardian!

If the pre-Islamic Scriptures had been corrupted, the Qur'an should not have ordered Muslims to:-

'Say (O Muslims): We believe in Allah and that which is revealed unto us and which was revealed unto Abraham, and Ishmael, and Isaac, and Jacob, and the tribes, and that which Moses and Jesus received, and that which the Prophets received from their Lord. We make no distinction between any of them, and unto him we have surrendered.'[7]

Documentary evidence

Numerous manuscript copies of all parts of the Bible written centuries before the time of Muhammad are available today. For example, the Dead Sea Scrolls, which were written before 68 AD contain most of every book of the Old Testament except one, Esther.[8] Also, some of the oldest Greek manuscripts of the entire New Testament which are available for research are the Codex Alexandrinus and the Codex Sinaiticus. These manuscripts date from the fourth and fifth centuries AD and may be studied in the British Museum in London. Another early manuscript is the Codex Vaticanus in the Vatican Library which is also from the same era as the other two manuscripts. In many great libraries, manuscripts of portions of the New Testament which date back to the second century may also be studied. The reliability of the present-day Bible may be verified by comparison with such documents as these.

Modern *bona fide* translations are basically the same in content as the documents current in Muhammad's time. They do not differ in any item of doctrine. God has preserved his word in the past and is able to preserve it in the future.

References

1. Qur'an 2:101, 3:23, 5:44, 40:53–54, 2:53, 21:48, 2:87, 5:46
2. Qur'an 28:43, cf. 3:3–4, 6:92
3. Qur'an 5:47
4. Qur'an 48:23
5. Isaiah 40:8
6. Qur'an 5:48
7. Qur'an 2:136
8. F.F. Bruce, *Second Thoughts on the Dead Sea Scrolls*, (Grand Rapids: Wm B. Eerdmans Publishing Co., 1964), p.28.

Chapter 3

The Inspiration of the Bible

The Bible was written over a long period by about forty different writers. They used three different languages and wrote on three different continents, and yet each part has the same thing to say about life's most controversial issues.

The Bible, as said before, is divided into two parts or 'Testaments'. The first part, the Old Testament, tells of God's dealings with the people of Israel. The second part, the New Testament, tells of the life of Jesus and his early followers, and includes letters written to help the early believers to hold fast to the teachings of Jesus.

God's word

The Bible is the inspired record of the revelation of God and not merely the chance compilation of a collection of human authors. It is God who directed his people.[1] He revealed his word in normal human literary forms such as historical narrative, poetry, proverbs, preaching and didactic teaching.

The testimony

'All Scripture is God-breathed and is useful for teaching, rebuking, correcting and training in righteousness, so that the man of God may be thoroughly equipped for every good work.'[2] To a Muslim this concept is not new, for it is a fundamental part of the teaching of the Qur'an.[3]

The Old Testament

We find the expression, 'Thus says the Lord' more than 3,800 times in the Old Testament. This makes clear the writers' belief that they spoke or wrote on God's behalf. We see that people of God, like Moses and David, were inspired by God. Although the Old Testament was written by many writers over many years, the dealings of God with men remain the same and so there is one overall picture which emerges.

Some important examples

The Bible records that God spoke to Moses: 'Now go; I will help you speak and will teach you what to say.'[4] This clearly teaches that Moses was inspired by God. God also spoke through David when he said, 'The Spirit of the Lord spoke through me; his word was on my tongue.'[5] We find similar evidence in the books of the prophets. For example, Jeremiah records that the Lord told him, 'I have put my words in your mouth.'[6]

There were many ways in which God made his will known in the Old Testament. He not only revealed his will through those who spoke his words, but also through the lives of those he touched; for example, the stories of Ruth and Job. All these, in very different ways, show the character of God and the way in which his love for his world reaches across time and space to care for individual people.

The verdict of Jesus

We also see that Jesus believed the Old Testament to be the word of God, when he said, 'Everything must be fulfilled that is written about me in the Law of Moses, the Prophets and the Psalms.'[7] These three divisions include all the Old Testament.

Jesus also endorsed the New Testament before it was written. Before his crucifixion, he told his disciples that when the Holy Spirit came, he would remind them of the things he had said. He promised that the Holy Spirit would guide them into all truth.[8] That is why the apostles testified that they spoke 'not in words taught us by human wisdom but in words taught by the Spirit.'[9]

The method

God used many methods to reveal his word to people. He gave his word to some by direct speech and to others through dreams and visions. His Holy Spirit guided them as they wrote or spoke using their full, normal faculties of intelligence and personal style. God gave them the freedom to write and speak through their own individual background, personality, vocabulary and style. If the writers of the Bible had been mere pens, instead of men, in the hands of God, its style and vocabulary would have been uniform. But such is not the case since we see their individuality coming through. Nevertheless behind them all is God and his revelation of himself. This gives the Bible unity.

> *Your word is a lamp to my feet and a light for my path* (Psalm 119:105)

Unity in the message

From beginning to end, there is one story of God's plan of salvation for mankind. There is one message throughout the Bible because there is one God and there is one mankind. God does not change, nor do the problems which face mankind. The greatest problem faced by man is: how to know God. God has made it plain that he is holy, completely holy, and that man does not live a holy life and so cannot know a holy God. The Bible addresses this universal problem. In its message the Bible says that God himself has provided the answer to it. We will consider this answer more fully in later chapters.

References

1. 2 Peter 1:20–2
2. 2 Timothy 3:16–17
3. Qur'an 2:136; 5:47; 10:95; 29:46
4. Exodus 4:12
5. 2 Samuel 23:2
6. Jeremiah 1:9
7. Luke 24:44
8. John 14:26; 16:13; 1 John 2:20,27
9. 1 Corinthians 2:13
10. John 14:6
11. 1 Timothy 2:4; 2 Peter 3:9

Chapter 4

The Accuracy of the Bible

Imagine what it would be like if there had been tape and video recorders, television and computers in the time of the prophets who were inspired by God and put his message down in writing. Today we would be able to see the original documents of their work or hear them talking, but we do not have such convenient assistance. What we do have, today, is their message which has been recorded in the Bible. The Bible was copied countless times and therefore some people ask, 'Can we be sure that the Bible has been preserved accurately?'

Original manuscripts

Some people say that they do believe in the Bible but not in the Bible we have today. One of the most frequent objections is that we do not have the very first manuscripts. People argue that scholars of the Bible

themselves agree that all the original manuscripts of
the Bible have perished.[1]

Whilst it may be true that all the original manuscripts of the Bible may have perished, we should bear
in mind that when the books of the Bible were origi-
nally written, there was no printing press available to
reproduce the copies. Each copy had to be written by
hand and relatively few copies could be made. In the
political conditions of the times it was inevitable that
some ancient manuscripts would be lost.

Old Testament

There are Hebrew Old Testament manuscripts
pre-dating Muhammad. Until 1947, the oldest
copy of the Old Testament available to us came
from around 900 AD. This is because a committee
of Jewish scholars did the same as Usman had
done. Then the Dead Sea Scrolls were found and
we got partial or complete copies of every book
of the Old Testament except Esther. They are all
dated before AD 70, and many can be dated to a
century earlier.

The Nash Payrus which contains sections of Exodus
and Deuteronomy is dated between 100 BC and AD 70.
There is also a collection of around 200 thousand
fragments of biblical texts in Hebrew and Aramaic,
other Jewish literature, religious and non-religious
texts available to us. It is called the Geniza Fragments
and dated to the AD 400s.

We also have available to us lists of Old Testament
books pre-dating Muhammad. For example Josephus
(AD90), a Jewish historian who wrote to Greeks and

Romans in defence of the Jewish nation and faith. We have the list of the Council of Jamnia (AD 75–117). At this assembly the Jewish elders in the course of their discussion listed Old Testament books. Later the Council of Laodicea (AD 363), a Christian church council was held to recognize the books of Scripture in the Old and New Testament. There are several other lists available to us in the writings of various early church fathers and all these lists show that the Jews were very serious and sure of the contents of the word they had received. Christians accepted the same Hebrew Scriptures as the word of God also.

There are many translations of the Old Testament in Greek, Latin and Syriac that pre-date Muhammad. They list the same books of the Old Testament that we have today. We are also aware that translations in Ethopic, Armenian, Georgian, Nubian etc. were available before the time of Muhammad.

New Testament

As for the New Testament, the evidence is even greater. We have about 4,500 manuscripts in whole and part. Comprehensive ones known as the Vatican, the Sinaitic and the Alexandrian uncials are world famous. They date back to AD 300–450.

There are 192 Greek New Testament manuscripts pre-dating Muhammad currently in existence and available for study.

Five Greek lectionaries, books that were used in church services and which contain Scripture portions, predating Muhammad are presently in existence.

We have available to us about 30 translations of the Greek New Testament from the time before Muhammad.

The earliest papyrus fragment containing portions of the verses of John 18:31–33, 37–38 is dated as AD 125 and is housed at the John Rylands Library in Manchester, England.

There are also two Greek fragments from the Dead Sea Scrolls that may very well be from the Gospel according to Mark and 1 Timothy. Both of these fragments date to before AD 70.

We also have the evidence from the early Christian leaders (AD 69–150). They wrote about the Bible and quoted in their writings portions of the Scriptures so that today almost the entire New Testament can be reconstructed from them. All these manuscripts do have variants in the text. However please do note that unlike Islam these variants have not been destroyed. They have been preserved, catalogued, studied and evaluated with the highest and most impartial degrees of scholarship. None of these variants affects any major or minor doctrine of the Christian faith.

In Old Testament times the Jews revered the sacred Scriptures deeply, as many do the Qur'an today. For this reason they would not allow any part of them to become dirty or ripped and thrown away like a piece of rubbish. They were committed to memory, accurately copied, and then the original was disposed of with great ceremony and dignity.

There are many other ancient books that have no original manuscripts available. Consider the Qur'an, for example. There is no known first manuscript nor contemporary copy available to us. As there were a number of differing copies with variant readings, Usman, the third successor of Muhammad, appointed a committee to collect and compile an official version of the Qur'an. When the task was completed, he ordered that the source copy and all previous copies should be burnt.[2] This does not mean that the Qur'an is not valid. But it does seem to be inconsistent to accept the Qur'an but reject the Bible when neither of them has their original manuscripts.

Accuracy of the text

We are not all historical scholars or archaeologists, but we can make up our own minds about the accuracy of the stories in a very simple way – by reading them! Read the stories of Jesus, for example, and see if there is not the ring of truth about them. Let us look at the healing of a blind man; it is in three of the four books of the life of Jesus (these accounts are called Gospels). The story is in Matthew 20:29–34, Mark 10:46–52, Luke 18:35–43. The blind man was begging, a fate common today in under-privileged places where such people are unable to earn their own living due to disease or disability. The disciples of Jesus were not very sympathetic, because they told the man to be quiet. Jesus, on the other hand, cared deeply for the man and healed him. Read the story yourself and see how the man's faith in Jesus made a difference to his life and filled him with joy.

Do we need the Torah and the Gospel?

Usually Muslim friends say that after all they do not
need the earlier Scriptures because the Qur'an contains
the earlier Scriptures and thus we do not need them.
However nowhere does the Qur'an say that it contains
the Torah and the Gospel. In fact the Qur'an claims
the contrary.

The Qur'an claims to be in the revealed books of the
former people (Surah 26:196). Further it claims to
have been given lest the Arabs make excuses that they
cannot understand the languages in which the earlier
books, the Torah and the Gospel were revealed (Surah
6:157,158).

Moreover, when Muhammad sought to establish
the authority of the Qur'an he placed it alongside the
Torah and the Gospel, '. . . bring ye a Book from Allah,
which is a better Guide than either of them, that I may
follow it! . . .' (Surah 28:49)

The Islamic faith requires that a Muslim should
believe in the books of the earlier prophets and this
principle makes the whole idea of abrogation wholly
contradictory to the teaching of the Qur'an which asks
Muslims to declare, 'We make no difference between
one and another of them . . .' (Surah 2:136).

Today, even with modern printing methods and
sophisticated systems, it is not unusual to see glaring
mistakes in published materials. So it is not difficult to
see how variant readings could have slipped unnoticed
into the Bible. All these manuscripts had to be produced by hand and no human hand is so exact or eye
so sharp as to preclude the possibility of errors. In most

modern translations these variant readings are noted in footnotes. The fact is that they are only few in number and they do not affect the teaching of the New Testament as a whole and this is what is most important.

Usually in their discussions Muslim friends raise the question of integrity about two short passages. They are the last twelve verses of Mark's gospel and John 8:1–11. Some manuscripts include them while others omit them.

These two passages make up not more than half a page of the Bible, the full length of which exceeds twelve hundred pages. We find no doctrine in these two passages that does not appear elsewhere in the New Testament. They are consistent with the text of the New Testament as a whole. If these variants are to be taken as proof of corruption in the Bible, the same standard should be applied to the Qur'an or any other book of that era claiming to be inspired or revealed.

References

1. Ahmad Deedat, *Is the Bible the Word of God?* (Durban: Islamic Propagation Centre, 1982), p. 64.
2. *Sahih Bukhari*, Vol.6, p. 479.

Chapter 5

The Accuracy of the Bible (2)

Archaeological findings

Archaeology is the scientific study of the remains of the past. The archaeologist studies the remains of ancient cities and houses and examines items like pots and tools found in the ruins. He tries to read any written records on stone, clay or other materials which have not decayed. Archaeologists have worked for many years in lands mentioned in the Bible. It is amazing the things which are constantly coming to light from their findings.

The art of writing pre-dates Moses

At one time scholars critical of the Bible said many things in the Bible could not have happened. Now archaeological discoveries have shown that the things mentioned in the Bible could have happened in the way they are described. For example: at one time it was thought that writing had not been invented in Moses' day, but archaeology has shown this assumption to be wrong.

Pontius Pilate

Until recently we knew about this Roman governor from the New Testament and from the writings of Josephus, Philo and Tacitus. It was in 1961 that a stone slab was discovered at Caesarea (about 65 miles from Jerusalem), inscribed with three names including those of Pilate and the emperor Tiberius.[1]

Customs of many years before Christ

Archaeological discoveries have shown that the customs of 2,000 years before Jesus fit the Bible's account of Abraham.[2] The Genesis account of Joseph in Pharaoh's court uses just the right technical terms and refers to practices followed in Egypt's royal court 1,800 years before Jesus.[3]

The city Tyre

Ezekiel, writing around 592-580 BC, foresaw the destruction of the city of Tyre.[4] This happened during the reign of Nebuchadnezzar of Babylon. Later on, Alexander the Great came and used the ruins of the mainland city to build a roadway to an island. The same prophecy also said that where the city once stood, fishermen would spread their nets, but the city would not be rebuilt.[5] Modern Tyre is not built where the old city stood. Even today, some 2,500 years after the prophecy, fishermen spread their nets on the rocky shore.

Destruction of Nineveh

The prophet Nahum, about 640 BC, wrote about the destruction and desolation of Nineveh. He prophesied that this capital of the Assyrian empire would be destroyed by an overwhelming flood.[6] He also said that the destruction would be total.[7] In about 612 BC, an enemy attacked the Assyrians outside Nineveh and the city was so completely destroyed that its ruins were not even located until the last century, about 2,400 years later. Many examples could be given but the above will serve to show that the Bible has an integrity and authenticity which means that we can read it with confidence.

Prophecies fulfilled

In biblical terms, prophecy is the revelation of God's truth about the past, present and future. These prophecies are often beyond human foresight and are remarkably detailed. The fulfilment of these prophecies in history is confirmation of God's inspiration of his prophets. There are many prophecies mentioned in the Bible. Many have been fulfilled and there are others which are still to be fulfilled. Here is just one example:

The Book of Isaiah is a prophetic book in the Old Testament and was written hundreds of years before Jesus was born. Yet as we read parts of it, we are struck by the way Jesus himself lived out the passages in that book. The beginning of chapter 53 (verses 1 to 3) speaks of how Jesus was rejected, and goes on to show that, because people didn't understand him, he was killed (verses 7 to 9). Yet God gave him a place of honour and greatness (verses 10 to 12).

Other prophets

There are some people today who claim to be able to foretell the future; but consider what they say. Often they are so vague as to be meaningless. The rest of their predictions are sometimes right and sometimes wrong, hardly a significant forecast! Biblical prophecy is different. What the Bible says will happen always takes place. Biblical prophecies are often about things that will happen hundreds of years after the person who made them has died. The fulfilled prophecies of the Bible are strong evidence that it is God's book because only God can reveal the future.

References

1. cf. Luke 3:1; Matthew 27:2; Mark 15:1–5; Luke 23:1; John 18:28–29
2. Genesis 12–25
3. Genesis 39–41
4. Ezekiel 26:3–21
5. Ezekiel 26:5,14
6. Nahum 2:6
7. Nahum 3:15

Chapter 6

The Abiding Word

There are Muslim friends who acknowledge that
the Torah, the Psalms, the Injil and the books of
the prophets were given by God. However some
say that these books which are all found in the
Bible are now *'mansukh'* – abrogated or can-
celled.[1] They claim that Muhammad's message,
the Qur'an, has replaced them all including the
Gospel of Jesus, and that Muhammad's message
will not be replaced until the day of judgement. It
is important to know that there is not a single
verse in the Qur'an to support this.

Does the Bible say that the Law or the Torah was
replaced by the Psalms? The truth is quite the opposite.
David says, 'The law of the Lord is perfect, reviving
the soul. The statutes of the LORD are trustworthy,
making wise the simple'.[2] Thus the Zabur (Psalms)
plainly confirms the Torah.

Did Jesus claim that the earlier revelations were

abrogated? We find him saying, 'Do not think that I have come to abolish the Law or the Prophets; I have not come to abolish them but to fulfil them'.[3]

Is it possible for the Injil to be abrogated? Jesus says, 'Heaven and earth will pass away, but my words will never pass away.'[4] No wonder the New Testament clearly reminds us, 'All men are like grass, and all their glory is like the flowers of the field; the grass withers and the flowers fall, but the word of the Lord stands for ever.'[5]

So there is no replacement of one message by another. Rather there is a building upon what has gone before, deepening it and making the will of God clearer.

Testimony of the Qur'an

There is no indication in the Qur'an that it has annulled the Bible. The only two places where the verb '*nasakha*' (to annul) is used, refer to certain verses of the Qur'an and not to the Bible.[6] In fact we find verses in the Qur'an which confirm the earlier Scripture – the Bible – and which ask Jews and Christians to abide by what is revealed in it.[7] How admirable of the Qur'an to tell us to abide by what we read in the Bible. The words of Jesus will never pass away. Jesus spoke truth to humanity in his day and, because humanity is still the same, that truth applies even today.

Animal sacrifices

Some may ask: 'Why don't Christians offer any

sacrifices to God, keep the Sabbath rest, or circumcise their children according to God's commandments in the Torah?'

The Old Testament tells us that when Adam and Eve sinned and were asked to leave God's presence, he commanded that sacrifices should be offered when people wanted to be accepted by him. We see that Abraham, Moses, David and many others offered such sacrifices. These were pictures of the one final sacrifice to be offered by the promised Saviour, Jesus. Details concerning his coming are prophesied in many of the earlier parts of the Bible. We will study these further in a later chapter.

In the Psalms, David prophesied, '. . . burnt offerings and sin offerings you did not require . . . Here I am, I have come . . . I desire to do your will . . .'[8] In the New Testament we see that Jesus fulfilled this prophecy by offering himself up, as a sacrifice, for us.[9]

Payments on account are needed only until the whole bill is settled and paid for. Likewise, these animal sacrifices were needed only until the sacrifice of Jesus had been offered. He has suffered once for all to bring us near to God.[10] Thus, when we believe in Jesus, God expects from us a faith which leads to a life of praise and good behaviour.[11]

The Sabbath & ceremonial laws

The Sabbath was appointed as a day of rest for man in remembrance of the fact that God completed the work of creation in six days. After believing in Jesus a Christian becomes a new creation. So there is another day to remember, the day upon which this was made possible. This is the first day of the week, the day on which Jesus was raised. Thus it is on this day that Christians rest and rejoice, gathering to worship and praise God.

Circumcision was the sign of the covenant God made with Abraham. Moses made its spiritual meaning clearer when he said: 'The Lord your God will circumcise your hearts and the hearts of your descendants, so that you may love him with all your heart and with all your soul, and live.'[12] Centuries later, God said through the prophet Jeremiah, 'The time is coming . . . when I will make a new covenant with the house of Israel . . . It will not be like the covenant I made with their forefathers . . . This is the covenant that I will make . . . I will put my law in their minds and write it on their hearts . . .'[13] This new covenant is recorded in the New Testament. This inner circumcision of the heart is the experience of every true Christian.

Outward forms of worship may be altered but God alone is to be worshipped. One prophet may die and another may come but God's words can never be treated as annulled. We see that the fullness of God's truth was not revealed to mankind all at once but, as the Bible puts it, 'In the past God spoke to our forefathers through the prophets at many times and in various ways, but in these last days he has spoken to us by his Son'.[14] Jesus came to complete God's mission once and for all. This message of God is not abrogated; it is everlasting.

Let us look at some eternal truths which Jesus taught us. Open your Bible at the New Testament and find the first of the accounts of the life of Jesus, called Matthew's Gospel. Turn to chapter 5 and begin reading at verse 1. These verses show the way to true happiness or blessing. They have been called 'The Beatitudes' for this reason.

Jesus teaches that heaven does not await the proud or arrogant, but those who humbly confess that they are poor in spirit and need God to teach them (verse 3). God reaches out, not to those who claim to know everything and delight in their own goodness, but to those who mourn their own inadequacies and weep for their own shortcomings (verse 4). It is the meek, or humble, who will inherit God's favour, not the proud and boastful (verse 5). Jesus says that a merciful heart receives mercy from God (verse 7). Purity begins in the heart and when a man's heart is pure he shall see God (verse 8).

It is not through hatred, anger and violence that we are seen as the children of God, but through making peace with ourselves, with those around us and with God. There is much more of this wonderful teaching. Surely this shows that the Injil is eternal, because it reveals eternal truth.

References

1. Tafsir Baidawi, on Qur'an 9:29
2. Psalm 19:7
3. Matthew 5:17
4. Matthew 24:35
5. 1 Peter 1:24–25
6. Qur'an 2:106; 22:51; cf. 16:101

 7. Qur'an 5:44–48
 8. Psalm 40:6–8
 9. Hebrews 10:6–10
10. 1 Peter 3:18
11. Hebrews 13:15–16
12. Deuteronomy 30:6
13. Jeremiah 31:31–33
14. Hebrews 1:1–2

Chapter 7

Prophecies about Jesus

God sees the end from the beginning. He sometimes reveals things which are to happen in the future, through prophecies. Some of the most amazing Bible prophecies are about Jesus; remember, for example, Isaiah 53, to which we have referred several times. These prophecies show that Jesus is truly the Messiah because he fulfilled them.

Long before Jesus was born, the Jewish people realized that there were many prophecies in the Scriptures about the Messiah. When Jesus arrived, he said to them, 'You diligently study the Scriptures because you think that by them you possess eternal life. These are the Scriptures that testify about me.'[1]

If you read the Gospel of Matthew, you will find at least 21 references to fulfilled prophecies! The whole of the New Testament clearly shows that it was Jesus who fulfilled these Old Testament prophecies. Let us examine just a few of them and their fulfilment.

Jesus to be born of a virgin

Hundreds of years before Christ, God spoke through the prophet Isaiah. 'The Lord himself will give you a sign: The virgin will be with child and will give birth to a son, and you will call him Immanuel.'[2] We see the fulfilment of this prophecy when Mary (i.e. Maryam) was visited by an angel who told her she would bear a son. All this took place to fulfil what God had promised.[3]

Jesus to be born in Bethlehem

Through the prophet Micah, God foretold that Jesus was to be born in Bethlehem.[4] This prophecy was well-known even to King Herod and his advisors. The New Testament tells us that Jesus was indeed born in Bethlehem in Judea.[5]

Jesus to perform miracles

Again, God said through the prophet Isaiah, '. . . your God will come . . . Then will the eyes of the blind be opened and the ears of the deaf unstopped. Then will the lame leap like a deer, and the mute tongue shout for joy.'[6] The Gospel according to Matthew confirms this prophecy in these words: 'Jesus went through all the towns and villages, teaching in their synagogues, preaching the good news of the kingdom and healing every disease and sickness.'[7]

Jesus to be crucified

The crucifixion of Jesus was not an accident or simply

a ghastly mistake. It was Jesus himself who laid down
his life. Why? Because God wanted to bring mankind
to himself. It was prophesied that Jesus, 'poured out
his life unto death, and was numbered with the transgressors. For he bore the sin of many, and made
intercession for the transgressors.'[8] When Jesus was
crucified, the Romans crucified two robbers with him,
one on his right and one on his left.[9]

Jesus' side to be pierced

'They will look on me, the one they have pierced.'[10]
These words were fulfilled in Jesus when one of the
soldiers pierced his side.[11]

Many more prophecies

Actually there are many more prophecies about Jesus
than are listed here. It was prophesied that Jesus was
to be betrayed by a friend and this is exactly what
happened.[12] In addition it was prophesied that Judas
would be paid thirty pieces of silver for this act of
betrayal and that he would later throw the money
down in God's house. The money was used to pay for
a potter's field[13] and this too was predicted accurately.
Judas was so sure he was doing right at the time but
he was full of bitter regret when he saw the outcome
of his actions.[14]

We can see from all of this that the Bible is not just
a collection of books. The common themes of God's
dealings with mankind and their response to him shine
through the whole Bible. This is particularly the case
with Jesus; the prophecies we have considered are like

signposts pointing the way to the coming Messiah. When Jesus came, he looked back to those same signposts and showed that they were true.[15] Like signposts, they can easily be misread. Jesus found that the Jews of his day had read the signs (prophecies) wrongly; they were expecting a victorious soldier or statesman rather than a humble preacher from the northern province of Galilee.

What do you think?

Some may say that the Old Testament was written after the New Testament in order to supply such accurate prophecies. This is just not possible. The Jews have guarded their Scriptures with the utmost care since the fourth century BC. They would never have tolerated interference with their holy book because this would have destroyed the whole basis of their faith and tradition.

The truth is that the Old Testament was already very widely circulated and even translated before the time of Jesus. A translation into the Greek language was already available in the second century BC. This is called the Septuagint and many copies are in museums today. It would be impossible to change the text of the Old Testament in such circumstances. Recently, pre-Christian copies of the Old Testament books have been discovered which contain the very same prophecies. These are the Dead Sea Scrolls which I mentioned in Chapter 4. Anyone who reads the Bible itself with an unprejudiced mind will be convinced of its truth.

References

1. John 5:39
2. Isaiah 7:14
3. Matthew 1:18,22–23
4. Micah 5:2
5. Matthew 2:1; Luke 2:4–7; John 7:42
6. Isaiah 35:4–6
7. Matthew 9:35; cf. Matthew 11:4–6
8. Isaiah 53:12
9. Matthew 27:38
10. Zechariah 12:10
11. John 19:34
12. Psalm 41:9; cf. John 13:18; Matthew 10:4
13. Zechariah 11:12
14. Matthew 26:15; Matthew 27:5,7
15. Augustine, a fifth century Christian, once said that the Bible is connected in this way: 'The New in the Old Concealed, the Old in the New Revealed'.

Chapter 8

Jesus the Messiah

Jesus is unique. We find that the whole Bible is really written about Jesus. He is the golden thread that runs from the promise of his coming in Genesis to the promise of his coming again in Revelation.[1] Muslims already know about Jesus' birth and his preaching of the Gospel of the Kingdom of God from reading the Qur'an.[2] Among them he is known as the Word of God and Spirit from him. In the Qur'an wherever Jesus is mentioned, his earthly patronymic identity as *Ibn Maryam* is also given, so he is known as *Al-Masih-u-Isa Ibn Maryam* – Jesus, the Christ, son of Mary. Like the Bible, the Qur'an gives testimony that God sent him as the sign of blessing for the nations of the earth (*Surah Imran & Surah Maryam*). God sent him as a sign and a mercy, to present Jesus as the '*Hujat ullah*' – Allah's proof, to the nations. The Qur'an witnesses to Jesus being the *Rahmat* (mercy) and *ayah* (sign) but it does not go into full details of the reason why God acted in such a way and what in fact the Qur'anic verse means when it says, *Wa kana amran Maqzia* – It is a matter (so) decreed (Surah 19:21). We can find the full details in the Bible.

His arrival on this earth

Jesus' birth took place at a time when many were waiting for the promised Messiah to arrive. King Herod was ruling in Jerusalem and when he heard about the birth of the 'King of the Jews', he tried to kill every young child in Bethlehem. Guided by God, Jesus and his family fled to Egypt. After Herod's death they returned to settle in Nazareth. The next mention of Jesus in the Gospel is when he was twelve years old. He went to the temple in Jerusalem and sat with the learned rabbis, talking to them about spiritual things.[3]

His mission

At the age of about thirty, Jesus started his ministry, preaching to people about the great things God had done for them. One day he met John the Baptist (*Hazrat Yahya*), a prophet of God. When John saw Jesus, he pointed to him and said to those around him, 'Look, the Lamb of God, who takes away the sin of the world!'[4] He was referring to the fact that Jesus was to be the sacrifice that God would provide, like the ram in the case of Abraham and his son, or the lambs sacrificed as sin offerings.[5]

Jesus, the Christ

The name 'Jesus' is itself important because of its meaning: 'the Lord saves'.[6] This name was given to him not by his family but by God himself. God was showing us that he planned to save us through the person of Jesus.

Jesus was also known as 'the Christ'. This word is the Greek equivalent of the Hebrew 'Messiah', which in Arabic is 'Al-Masih', and means 'anointed'. In Hebrew culture, a person was anointed with oil as a sign that he was being called to some special task. The Hebrews anointed their kings and priests.

His ministry as teacher

In Jesus' day the Jewish teachers had made their religion a mechanical and outward thing, but Jesus taught that God was more interested in men's hearts and their inward motives.[7] All people were important to him, whether they were part of a crowd or met him individually. They felt that Jesus was different from other rabbis. His followers soon learned that he was not just a teacher; he was also 'Lord'. Jesus accepted both titles, saying, 'You call me "Teacher" and "Lord", and rightly so, for that is what I am.'[8]

The title he most often took upon himself was 'Son of Man'. This is a most significant title. In the Old Testament it was used in two totally different ways. Ezekiel, an Old Testament prophet, is described as a Son of man.[9] The context makes it clear that Ezekiel's humanity is being emphasized. However, in the book of Daniel, the same phrase takes on another meaning[10].

In this context someone of great spiritual power, even divine, is being referred to. Jesus used this title for himself to show people the two aspects of his nature.

Many people recognized something else that was unique about Jesus. Their teachers used to quote others as their authority for any ruling they made, but they realized that Jesus was different. They regarded him as 'one who had authority, and not as their teachers of the law'.[11] Also other prophets used to say, 'The Lord your God says, . . .' but Jesus said, 'I tell you . . .' or 'Truly, I tell you . . .'

One of the main teachings of Jesus was about God's kingdom. 'The time has come,' he proclaimed, 'The kingdom of God is near. Repent and believe the good news!'[12] By this he wanted to teach us that God is still in control and that he wants all men to come back to himself. This does not mean that man has no freedom of choice.[13] Jesus' teaching was that whoever believes in him may have eternal life.

His miracles

Jesus performed miracles in response to particular needs. He cured people who were ill.[14] He fed thousands of people.[15] He even calmed the waves.[16] No wonder then, that when Jesus cured a paralysed man, just by saying, '. . . take up your mat and go home . . .', the response of the crowd was: 'We have seen remarkable things today.'[17] Those who followed him marvelled, 'What kind of man is this? Even the winds and the waves obey him!'[18] Gradually his followers came to understand that Jesus was no ordinary person.

His influence

Jesus was very much welcomed by ordinary people. The majority of the religious leaders, however, did not like him, because he was a friend of tax collectors, sinners and religious outcasts.[19] Yet many of these outcasts recognized their need to repent and follow Jesus.[20] He invited everyone to realize their need of God and come to know him personally. The purity of Jesus' life is an example for us all to follow. He could challenge his enemies by saying, 'Can any of you prove me guilty of sin?'[21] No one did or could. It was because of Jesus' sinlessness that he was able to accomplish the great purpose for which he came.

(Further study on the subject of this great purpose is found in Chapter 18.)

References

1. Genesis 3:15; Revelation 22:20
2. Matthew 1:18; Qur'an 19:16–35
3. Luke 2:41–50
4. John 1:29
5. Genesis 22:13; Leviticus 6:24–30
6. Matthew 1:21
7. Matthew 5:21–30
8. John 13:13
9. Ezekiel 3:3
10. Daniel 7:13–14
11. Matthew 7:28–29
12. Mark 1:14–15

13. Matthew 13:1–23; Joel 2:32
14. Mark 5:35–42; Luke 17:11–19
15. Mark 6:30–46; 8:1–10
16. Matthew 8:23–27; Mark 4:35–39
17. Luke 5:26
18. Matthew 8:27
19. Matthew 9:9–13
20. Luke 19:1–10
21. John 8:46

Chapter 9

The Crucifixion Factor

It may seem hard to understand why such a godly prophet who taught with such authority and wisdom should die a horrible death on a cross. After all, crucifixion was a method of execution used for common criminals. In fact, this has offended some people so much that they will not accept its truth. However the Bible tells us that Jesus did not come only to teach and to heal. His main mission was to open the door of forgiveness for all mankind by giving his life on the cross.

One of his apostles, Peter, was very upset when he heard Jesus' predicting his own death on the cross. However, Peter later realized that this was God's choice. All this had been prophesied by Isaiah centuries before Jesus, as we saw in chapter 4[1]. The fact that one third of the Gospel is devoted to Jesus' death on the cross and to his resurrection shows just how important these events were.

The plot

Some of the Jews did believe in Jesus and put their faith
in him. However, others were violently opposed to
him; these were mostly the religious leaders of the day
who regarded Jesus as a threat to their status and
power. So, just before the annual Passover festival,
they arrested Jesus and accused him of blasphemy.
They handed him over to the Roman authorities,
changing the charge to sedition, that is, speaking
against Caesar.

Jesus' trial, death & resurrection

The Roman governor, Pilate, delivered Jesus to
death in spite of having judged him completely
innocent, three times.[2] He was crucified and, after
six hours hanging on the cross, he died. If Jesus
had died on the cross and then remained in the
grave, it would have meant that he was neither the
Messiah nor the promised one. We know that in
those days many people were crucified. However,
Jesus rose again on the third day, after being dead
and buried.[3] For some forty days, Jesus was seen
alive by various people and later he was taken
into heaven before their eyes.[4]

The heart of the matter

The Christian claim is that, '. . . Christ died for our
sins according to the Scriptures.'[5] But it is on this point
that there is conflict. The Jews deny that Jesus was the
Messiah. They say that Jesus may have died on the

cross but it would be far-fetched to think he rose from the dead. Orthodox Islam, on the other hand, goes further and denies that Jesus was even crucified.[6] Yet it believes him to be the Messiah, accepts his bodily ascension and predicts his second coming.

The Ahmadiyya sect, on the other hand, accepts that Jesus was crucified, but says he merely swooned on the cross, revived in the tomb and eventually died in Kashmir at the age of 120.[7] It would be most unfair and uncharacteristic of God to allow Jesus to die in such a way if there was no point or reason for it. There was a most important reason, however, which makes the death of Jesus not only understandable, but even necessary!

God is holy, but man is not. How can the death of Jesus help solve this problem? Isaiah 53:4–6 and likewise many verses in the New Testament show us why Jesus died.[8] He did not die as punishment for his own sin; he died because of your sin and mine. He carried our wrongdoing.[9] He took our punishment. He received in his body the results of the many wrong things we have done.

An exchange took place on the cross. Try to imagine all the guilt, wrong and evil being taken from you and me and put upon Jesus. Look at Isaiah 53: 4–6 again with this in mind and ask God to help you to see the truth of it in your heart.

Can you see now how this solves the greatest problem which mankind has – how to come to have personal friendship with God? The solution was not that we should try to reach him by our good deeds; our good deeds hopefully outweighing our bad deeds on

God's scales. No! Jesus completely removed everything on the bad side of the scales! He took upon himself all the evil we do. Jesus received what we deserve – that is, the punishment for sin.[10]

Now we can begin to understand why Jesus had to die. When Jesus died it was God reaching down to deal with a problem which man could not solve on his own. 'For God so loved the world that he gave his one and only Son . . .'[11] If we deny the crucifixion, it means that Christ was a deceiver, for he spoke about his death beforehand. He told his followers that he must go to Jerusalem and suffer many things at the hands of the elders, chief priests and scribes, and be killed and raised again on the third day.[12] On another occasion he said that he had come to give his life as a ransom for many.[13]

In the Qur'an there is only one reference to Jesus' crucifixion and that is ambiguous,[14] but in the New Testament we have reference after reference that Jesus did die on the cross. Jesus himself later testified to this truth by saying, 'I am the Living One; I was dead, and behold I am alive for ever and ever!'[15]

We see that, according to the prophecies of the Scriptures, Jesus is the only Saviour. The Bible declares, 'Salvation is found in no one else, for there is no other name under heaven given to men by which we must be saved.'[16]

The substitution theory

Some maintain that it is an awful disgrace for a prophet to be killed. Thus, for Jesus to have been crucified would be intolerable. Yet, in the Qur'an and the Bible it is recorded that the Jews slew several innocent prophets.[17]

Some Muslims argue that someone else must have been crucified as a substitute. It was not Jesus who was executed but another, who was miraculously substituted . . . for him.[18] Some claim that Judas Iscariot was slain in his place; others say that it was Simon of Cyrene.

The Qur'an does not mention any name. If we say that it was Judas Iscariot on the cross and that God made his face look like that of Jesus to mislead people this would mean that God is one who deceives and such a notion is intolerable. If it was true Judas would surely have protested. This theory engages God in a cheap deceptive charade.

Let us take Simon of Cyrene. Some say that, since he was carrying the cross of Jesus, people confused him with Jesus and so he was crucified by mistake! But again we have to ask ourselves this question: 'How could Jesus, the true Prophet of God, have allowed such a terrible deception?' It is unthinkable. We see that this theory implies that God is the author of fraud.

The swoon theory

The Ahmadiyya Movement teaches that Jesus was indeed crucified but that he survived the cross, was taken down in a swoon and presumed to be dead. In the coolness of the grave he recovered and later went to India, where he preached until his death at the age of 120. Though this theory is part of the Ahmadiyya faith it is also put forward by some Muslims who are not of this sect.[19]

Jesus preached in Jerusalem, Judea and Samaria for only three and a half years and performed many miracles there. History books contain information about this and there are many evidences of his life and ministry there, even today. Isn't it strange then that, though he is supposed to have preached in India for between eighty and ninety years, there is no evidence of anyone believing in him. Research indicates that the supposed grave of Jesus is actually that of Prince Yuz Asef!

To believe this theory would mean that the Old Testaments prophets who prophesied about Jesus were liars. Jesus himself predicted his death on the cross and resurrection from the dead. Following the swoon theory would mean that Jesus was also a liar or one who did not know his mission.

References

1. Isaiah 52:13–53:12
2. John 18:28–19:25
3. Matthew 27, 28
4. Acts 1:1–9
5. 1 Cor 15: 3–4
6. Qur'an 4:157–158
7. Mirza Ghulam Ahmad, *Jesus in India* (Rabwah: The Ahmadiyya Foreign Missions, n.d.), pp.59–60.
8. Mark 10:45; 2 Cor 5:21; 1 Peter 2:21–25; cf. Rom. 3:21–31
9. Other meaning of the text is 'shouldered'.

10. Ezekiel 18:20
11. John 3:16
12. Matthew 16:21
13. Matthew 20:28
14. Qur'an 4:157
15. Revelation 1:18
16 Acts 4:12
17. Qur'an 4:155
18. Maulana Abdul Majid Daryabadi, Holy Qur'an, (Karachi: Taj Co. Ltd., 1970), Vol. I, p.96-A.
19. Ahmad Deedat, *Crucifixion or Crucifiction*, (Birmingham: Islamic Propagation, 1986)
20. Isaiah 53:7–12

Chapter 10

The Risen Jesus!

Jesus was raised from the dead in fulfilment of prophecy, as he had predicted. His followers were astonished. He had raised others from the dead; now he had victoriously defeated death. He appeared to the apostles that first Sunday evening, in an upper room in Jerusalem. For some reason one apostle, Thomas, was not there. When he was told that Jesus had risen, he refused to believe it. He said, 'Unless I see the nail marks in his hands and put my finger where the nails were, and put my hand into his side, I will not believe it.'[1]

Just one week later when all the apostles, including Thomas, were present, Jesus appeared to them and said, 'Peace be with you!' He said to Thomas, 'put your finger here; see my hands. Reach out your hand and put it into my side. Stop doubting and believe.'[2] There was no need for Thomas to check further. He cried out, 'My Lord and my God!' Jesus' response was,

'Because you have seen me, you have believed; blessed are those who have not seen and yet have believed.'[3]

Jesus had promised his followers that he would be killed, but would then rise again.[4] After the resurrection he reminded them, 'This is what I told you while I was still with you: Everything must be fulfilled that is written about me in the Law of Moses, the Prophets and the Psalms.'[5]

A few days after Jesus' ascension, Peter boldly testified to a crowd about Jesus, saying, 'God raised him from the dead, freeing him from the agony of death, because it was impossible for death to keep its hold on him.'[6]

Attacks

From the New Testament it is very clear that if Christ had not been raised, our faith would be useless. We would all be lost. There would be no hope of salvation [Please read 1 Corinthians 15:14–19]. From the day that Jesus rose until now, opponents have recognized the vital significance of this event and thus have tried to discredit it.

The sign of Jonah

On one occasion during Jesus' ministry on earth the Pharisees asked him to give them a miraculous sign to prove himself. Jesus replied, ' . . . for as Jonah was three days and three nights in the belly of a huge fish, so the Son of Man will be three days and three nights in the heart of the earth.'[7] Therefore, some argue that since Jonah was alive in the belly of the fish, then Jesus must also have been alive in the tomb.[8] However, the text goes on to say that 'one greater than Jonah is here' (verse 41) and 'one greater than Solomon is here' (verse 42) It is easy to see many differences between the two situations:

1. Jonah was an unwilling messenger whereas Jesus had chosen to do his Father's will.
2. Jonah's mission was to non-Jews but Jesus came for all, including the house of Israel.
3. Jonah's fate in the sea was uncertain whereas Jesus was to be executed by the most efficient civil and military power the world had ever known.
4. Jonah preached and both king and people repented, but Jesus' message was not received by the officials persecuting him.

Jesus was comparing the length of time he was to spend in the tomb with that spent by Jonah in the fish. The similarity between the two events does not extend any further. In addition, Jesus goes on to say that he is much greater than Jonah and, therefore, his resurrection was to be a much greater miracle than Jonah's survival in the fish. If he had simply swooned, there would have been no miracle at all.

The circumstances

Before Jesus was crucified, he was beaten terribly. Many watched him die, including soldiers who knew death well. One soldier stuck a spear into Jesus' side to make sure he was dead. His body was taken down from the cross and wrapped in grave clothes. The people who did this knew that he was dead and they put the body into a cave that had been carved into the solid rock to make a tomb. An enormous heavy stone was put in front of the tomb. It was sealed by the Roman officials, and a guard of Jewish soldiers was set to watch it.

Why did the people who killed Jesus put a guard outside his tomb? We do not usually send soldiers to guard a dead body! The answer is given in the Bible. Jesus had said that he would be killed and buried, and would come to life once again on the third day. The soldiers were told to guard the tomb because the authorities were afraid that Jesus' disciples would come and steal his body. Read for yourself: Matthew 12:38–40; 16:21; 17:22–23; 20:18–19; 26:32; 27:63; Mark 9:9–10,31; 10:33–34; 14:28,58; Luke 9: 22–23; John 2:19–22; 12:32–33; 14:1–16:33.

In spite of everything, the tomb was open and empty on the third day. There had been an earthquake. The great stone had been removed, and the soldiers had become unconscious. The grave clothes were there but Jesus' body was not. Neither the Roman nor the Jewish authorities were able to produce the body and prove that Jesus was dead. When the witnesses to the resurrection spoke up, they had no answer to give.

The witness report

Later Jesus was seen alive by many people. Here is the list of people that the Bible gives:-

Two Marys	(Matthew 28:10)
Simon Peter	(Luke 24:34)
Two unnamed disciples	(Luke 24:13–35)
Mary Magdalene	(John 20:10–17)
Ten apostles	(John 20:19–24)
Ten apostles with Thomas	(John 20:26–29)
The apostles at the ascension	(Acts 1:9–10)
Over 500 at one time	(1 Corinthians 15:6)

All these people knew Jesus very well and could not have been fooled. Some may ask how we know that these witnesses were not lying? One reason is because their lives were so dramatically changed after Jesus' ascension. The disciples who were so afraid and ran away when Jesus was arrested, suddenly became brave! The Bible tells us how Peter and John and the others faced the very people who had killed Jesus and yet refused to obey them. They preached not only to the crowds, but also to the very same leaders who had plotted to kill Jesus.[9]

A plea

Dear friend! Yes, we believe that Jesus really was raised from the dead. He himself said, 'I am the Living One; I was dead, and behold I am alive for ever and ever!'[10] Indeed he can save people like you and me from our sins. You and I live in a society in which many people no longer think about their destiny. Let us be aware of the fact that there is life beyond death. It is important to think about that future now. The Bible declares that if we put our trust in Jesus and obey his commands, we will be raised as Jesus was and forever live a joyful new life with God the Almighty, the Loving and Merciful in heaven.

References

1. John 20:25
2. John 20:27
3. John 20:28–29
4. Mark 9:31
5. Luke 24:44
6. Acts 2:24
7. Matthew 12:39–40
8. Ahmad Deedat, *What was the sign of Jonah?* (Birmingham: Islamic Propagation, 1985), p. 6.
9. Acts 4:9–12
10. Revelation 1:18

Chapter 11

The Person of Jesus

You have already learnt a number of things about Jesus that were probably new to you. You also saw how Muslims and Christians share the belief that Jesus is the prophet of God; he is the Word and Spirit of God. Now let us consider the person of Jesus in greater depth.

In Jewish history before Jesus, miracles had been mostly associated with prophets. The Qur'an ascribes to Moses similar miracles to those mentioned in the Bible. Moses had performed miracles, and so had other prophets. Now as people saw Jesus performing miracles, their natural response was to think that he was a prophet. On other occasions they exclaimed that a great prophet had appeared among them.[1]

The Bible states that after Jesus miraculously fed a crowd of more than 5,000 people, using five loaves of bread and two small fish, the people said, 'Surely this is the Prophet who is to come into the world.'[2]

The Prophet they were referring to was someone that Moses had said would come. Jesus certainly claimed that he was 'the Prophet'. He told the unbelieving Jews, 'If you believed Moses, you would believe me, for he wrote about me.'[3] The question that remains is, '*Was he more than a prophet?*'

Jesus' sinless life

From the time of his birth he remained innocent and pure. In the Bible and in the Qur'an several prophets like Abraham, Moses and David asked God for forgiveness, but there is no verse which says that Jesus ever asked for forgiveness. He challenged his enemies openly: 'Can any of you prove me guilty of sin?'[4] No one was able to point out any fault in him. Even at his trial before the Roman governor, Pilate was compelled to admit, 'I find no basis for a charge against him'.[5]

It is very easy to claim that one is sinless, but the proof must surely come from the testimony of others. Jesus' friends who lived with him, have the greatest testimony of all. Peter quotes a verse from the Old Testament with reference to Jesus: 'He committed no sin, and no deceit was found in his mouth.'[6] It says elsewhere that Jesus was 'tempted in every way, just as we are – yet was without sin'.[7]

What Jesus taught others, he lived out completely. Jesus' teaching in 'The Sermon on the Mount' (Matthew 5–7) is a reflection of the pure life he led. His extraordinary claim was that he fulfilled the law of the Old Testament.

Titles of Jesus in the Qur'an

The Qur'an talks about Jesus in fifteen surahs. He is called *Isa* which occurs 25 times and is often interpreted as 'Jesus' in English translations of the Qur'an. In 11 places he is referred to as *Al-Masih* (the Christ, the Messiah). Elsewhere, 23 times, he is spoken of as *Ibn-Maryam* (son of Mary). He is also called *the servant* or *slave* of God.

Surah	Isa	Al-Masih	Ibn Maryam
2:87,136,253	3	0	2
3:45,52,55,59,84	5	1	1
4:157,163,171,172	3	3	2
5:17,46,72,75,78,110–116	6	5	10
6:85	1	0	0
9:30,31	0	2	1
19:34	1	0	1
23:50	0	0	1
33:7	1	0	1
42:13	1	0	0
43:57,63	1	0	1
57:27	1	0	1
61:6,14	2	0	2

His authority over sin

It is believed that only God can forgive sins. We see that Jesus had the same authority. One day Jesus was teaching in a house. Some people came carrying a paralysed man on a mat. They tried to take him into the house but because it was very crowded they could not find a way in. So they went up and removed some of the roof to let the man down to where Jesus was.

When Jesus saw their faith, he said to the paralysed man, 'Friend, your sins are forgiven.' The man must have been shocked to hear this. The Jewish leaders who were also present said to themselves, 'Who is this fellow who speaks blasphemy? Who can forgive sins but God alone?'

Jesus knew what they were thinking, and asked them, 'Which is easier? to say, "Your sins are forgiven", or to say, "Get up and walk?" ' To show them that he had the authority to forgive sins, he said to the paralysed man, 'I tell you, get up, take your mat and go home.' Immediately he stood up in front of them, took his mat and went home praising God.[8]

Another time Jesus said to a woman, 'Your sins are forgiven . . . Go in peace.'[9] She also was healed as a sign to confirm her being forgiven. Not only had he authority to forgive sin, but Jesus had control over the normal workings of nature as well. People were amazed at his power and exclaimed, 'Even the winds and the waves obey him!'[10]

When we think about Jesus' works, we see the unlimited authority he has: he healed the sick by a word, or by his touch. He also gave this authority to his apostles and they performed miracles in his name. Jesus himself once said, 'You may ask me for anything in my name, and I will do it.'[11]

Jesus, the Lord of resurrection

There was a man called Lazarus who had died, and had been buried for four days. Jesus came up to his grave and shouted: 'Lazarus, come out!', and the dead

Lazarus came out alive and well![12]

Jesus claimed: 'I am the resurrection and the life. He who believes in me will live, even though he dies.'[13] In other places the extraordinary claim is made that it is only through Jesus that we can be forgiven and saved from eternal destruction.[14] We therefore see that his deeds proved his claims. He was more than a prophet. What do you think?

References

1. Luke 7:11–17
2. John 6:14
3. John 5:46 (cf. Deuteronomy 18:15–22)
4. John 8:46; Qur'an 38:23–24; 28:15–16; 26:82
5. John 18:38;19:4,6
6. 1 Peter 2:22 (cf. Isaiah 53:9)
7. Hebrews 4:15
8. Luke 5:17–26
9. Luke 7:36-50
10. Matthew 8:23–27
11. John 14:14
12. John 11: 1–44
13. John 11:25
14. John 14:6, Acts 4:12, Hebrews 7:25

Chapter 12

Jesus, the Son of Man

Jesus very often referred to himself as 'the Son of Man', using this title more than any other during his ministry. At the beginning of his ministry, he used it when addressed by a new disciple called Nathaniel. He said, 'I tell you the truth, you shall see heaven open, and the angels of God ascending and descending on the Son of Man'.[1]

He used it for the last time before the Jewish high priest, on the night before his crucifixion. He said to him, '. . . in the future you will see the Son of Man sitting at the right hand of the Mighty One and coming on the clouds of heaven'.[2]

There are many places in which Jesus seems to have used the title 'Son of Man' intentionally. Once when he was talking about the cost of people following him, he said, 'Foxes have holes and birds of the air have nests, but the Son of Man has no place to lay his head.'[3] What does this title mean? Does it simply tell us about the humanity of Jesus, that Jesus was emphasizing his humanity? *Was the 'Son of Man' just a human being?*

If you continue to study the various uses of the term 'Son of Man' in the New Testament, you will find (as we saw in the previous chapter) that Jesus is highlighting his God-given authority. Many of the learned Jews understood why Jesus was using such a title. For example, when talking about the end of the world, Jesus said, 'At that time the sign of the Son of Man will appear in the sky, and all the nations of the earth will mourn. They will see the Son of Man coming on the clouds of the sky, with power and great glory.'[4] On hearing a similar statement at Jesus' trial, the high priest of the Jews tore his clothes and said, 'He has spoken blasphemy!'[5] He reacted in such a way because according to Jewish teaching only God could do that. See for example Psalm 104:3.

A great prophet

Jewish listeners understood that Jesus was quoting directly from a well-known prophecy in the Old Testament, which had been given to the prophet Daniel in a vision.

'In my vision at night I looked, and there before me was one like a son of man, coming with the clouds of heaven. He approached the Ancient of Days (God) and was led into his presence. He was given authority, glory and sovereign power; all peoples, nations and men of every language worshipped him. His dominion is an everlasting dominion that will not pass away, and his kingdom is one that will never be destroyed.'[6]

The term 'Son of Man' in these writings is firmly linked with Jesus, who will come with the clouds of heaven. He will have complete authority over all people and nations. Quite obviously, the Son of Man is a glorious person, the embodiment of human perfection and honour.

In the Bible we find the expression 'son of man' also used in a general sense denoting humanity.[7] However when Jesus used this title for himself, it was in an exclusive sense, meaning that he is the ultimate Son of Man, the one who was seen by the prophet Daniel in his vision.

The purpose

As the Son of Man, Jesus gave his life for humanity, and afterwards was lifted up by God to glory in the heavens, to reign with him in wondrous majesty over all the sons of men. Jesus spoke about his death on the cross, his burial, and resurrection to his disciples, 'The Son of Man will go just as it is written about him'.[8] He was referring to Psalm 22, Psalm 69 and Isaiah 53.

On various occasions he brought out the other aspect of the Son of Man; showing himself to be a humble man serving his fellow men, and finally laying down his life for them. 'The Word' – *Kalima or Kalam* – voluntarily took on the form of a servant, not only to serve God, but even to serve his fellow men. He said 'The Son of Man did not come to be served, but to serve, and to give his life as a ransom for many.'[9]

Some of those who are opposed to the message of Christ, think of his crucifixion as an insult, but Jesus spoke of it as a means of being glorified. For example, shortly before his crucifixion he said to his disciples, 'The hour has come for the Son of Man to be glorified. I tell you the truth, unless a grain of wheat falls to the ground and dies, it remains only a single seed. But if it dies, it produces many seeds.'[10]

The third day after Jesus had died on the cross, God raised him from the dead, and forty days later, God lifted him up to glory in the heavens. One day Jesus will return to receive those who belong to him.[11]

> *The Son of Man did not come to be served, but to serve, and to give his life as a ransom for many.* (Matthew 20:28)

So we see that Jesus, the Son of Man, is unique among men, the One who has been given authority, glory and sovereign power and who will be worshipped by all people everywhere.

References

1. John 1:51
2. Matthew 26:64
3. Matthew 8:20
4. Matthew 24:30
5. Matthew 26: 64,65
6. Daniel 7:13–14
7. Job 25:6; Psalms 8:4; Isaiah 51:12
8. Matthew 26:24; cf. John 12:32–34
9. Matthew 20:28
10. John 12:23–24
11. 1 Thessalonians 4:16–17

Chapter 13

Jesus, the Promised Messiah

Among Muslims and many others Jesus is generally known by the title Messiah. In the Qur'an Jesus alone is called the Messiah – *Al-Masih*. Eleven times he is given this title and occasionally he is referred to by this title without his name. However, the Qur'an does not give an explanation as to why Jesus was called the Messiah.

The title 'Messiah' is extremely important to Christians and Jews; and we think it should be important also to Muslims because of the references to it in the Qur'an. The English word 'Christ' comes from the Greek word '*Christos*'. The word 'Messiah' comes from Hebrew. Both words mean the same – 'the Anointed One' or 'the One set apart for a special purpose'.

In the Old Testament this word is sometimes applied in a subordinate sense and thus could refer to an anointed priest or leader.[1] It was also given to the

prophets of God.[2] In addition it was given to the
Persian king Cyrus who was anointed by God to
prepare the way for the rebuilding of the city and the
temple of Jerusalem after its destruction by an earlier
king, Nebuchadnezzar.[3] This title became more important when it was revealed to Daniel that the Messiah
would come after the rebuilding of Jerusalem.[4] Evi-
dently, it became the accepted title of the one who was
to be the mighty deliverer and the ruler of God's
kingdom. Not only Daniel, but also prophets like
Isaiah, Micah, Zechariah and several others spoke
frequently of his coming.[5]

Jesus, the promised Messiah

Christians believe that Jesus is the Messiah. Jesus
testified that he was the Messiah. The Jews were
expecting a military leader who would drive out all
foreign powers from their land and set up the kingdom
of Israel, whereas Jesus told them that he came not 'to
be served, but to serve, and to give his life as a ransom
for many'.[6]

The testimony of the angel

When an angel appeared to Mary to tell her that she
was going to give birth to a son, he said, 'You are to
give him the name Jesus, because he will save his people
from their sins.'[7] It was no accident that Jesus received
this name which means 'the Lord saves'. After Jesus'
birth an angel appeared to some shepherds looking
after their flocks near Bethlehem. They were terrified,
but the angel said, 'Do not be afraid. I bring you good

news of great joy that will be for all the people. Today in the town of David a Saviour has been born to you; he is Christ the Lord.'[8]

The testimony of a disciple

One day Jesus asked his disciples, 'Who do you say I am?' One of them, Peter, replied that he was indeed the Messiah of God. Jesus told him that this recognition was from God, but warned him not to tell anyone.[9] This was because Jesus knew many people misunderstood the role of the Messiah. Immediately after Peter's declaration, Jesus began to talk of how he would suffer and give up his life. He was underlining the fact that the Messiah was to be a suffering Messiah and not one with a sword in his hand and ruling a worldly kingdom.[10]

The testimony of Jesus

One day, far away from the big towns and cities, at the side of a well in the despised area of Samaria, Jesus chose to reveal that he was the Messiah to a person who was an outcast in the eyes of the Jews – a Samaritan woman. After Jesus had told her that God was looking for people who would worship him in spirit and truth, the woman said, 'I know that Messiah is coming. When he comes, he will explain everything to us.' Jesus declared, 'I who speak to you am he.'[11]

After Jesus had fulfilled his mission and ascended to heaven, the apostles understood the whole plan and did not hesitate to tell others, using this title for Jesus. For example, Peter told the Jews at Pentecost, 'God

has made this Jesus, whom you crucified, both Lord
and Christ.'[12]

The Messiah & the Son of God

It is very significant to see that in the Christian Scriptures the title 'Christ' or 'Messiah' *(Masih)* is used in
parallel with the title 'Son of God'. Very often these
two titles are found together.

Jewish believers called Jesus both the Messiah and
the Son of God. Peter mentioned both titles together.
He said, 'You are the Christ (the Messiah), the Son of
the living God.'[13] Martha, the sister of Lazarus, the
man whom Jesus raised from the dead, used the two
titles together in her expression of belief in Jesus. Her
words were, 'I believe that you are the Christ (Messiah), the Son of God, he who was to come into the
world.'[14]

In Mark we read, 'The beginning of the Gospel
about Jesus Christ, the Son of God'.[15] In John we also
read, '. . . Jesus is the Christ (Messiah), the Son of God,
. . .'[16]

We also see that during Jesus' trial, the Jewish high
priest used both titles when asking Jesus if he was the
Messiah. 'I charge you under oath by the living God:
tell us if you are the Christ (the Messiah), the Son of
God.' In confirming the claim, Jesus added, 'In the
future you will see the Son of Man sitting at the right
hand of the Mighty One and coming on the clouds of
heaven.'[17]

In saying this, Jesus was referring to his second
coming. The Jews were right in their belief that the

Messiah was to come from heaven and would establish the kingdom of God, but they failed to distinguish between the two comings of the Messiah. At his first advent Jesus was to be a suffering Messiah and at his second coming he is to be the victorious Mighty King and Judge.

References

1. Leviticus 4:3; 2 Samuel 1:14
2. Psalm 105:15
3. Isaiah 45:1
4. Daniel 9:25
5. Isaiah 11:1–5; 42:1; Micah 5:2; Zechariah 6:12–13
6. John 4:26; Mark 10:42–45; Matthew 20:28; John 13:15–16
7. Matthew 1:21
8. Luke 2:8–14
9. Matthew 16:13–20; Luke 9:20–21
10. Matthew 16:21–28
11. John 4:25–26
12. Acts 2:36; 1 Corinthians 1:1–3; Hebrews 3:6; 1 Peter 4:1
13. Matthew 16:16
14. John 11:27
15. Mark 1:1
16. John 20:31
17. Matthew 26:63–64

Chapter 14

Jesus, the Son of God

Some people think that the Christian belief in the Fatherhood of God and the Sonship of Jesus rests on the belief that God has a wife. The question is put in this way: 'How can God have a Son when he has no wife, no consort?'

The Father & the Son

The Bible nowhere claims such a literal sonship for Jesus; it does not say that Jesus is the Son of God in the sense that God had a wife. In the Bible, God the Father and Jesus the Son are to be understood in a spiritual sense. Christians did not invent these titles. It was Jesus himself who introduced God to us as the Father. He taught his disciples to pray, as follows, 'Our Father in heaven, hallowed be your name, your kingdom come, your will be done on earth as it is in heaven. Give us today our daily bread. Forgive us our debts, as we also have forgiven our debtors. And lead us not into temptation, but deliver us from the evil one, for yours is the kingdom and the power and the glory for ever. Amen.'[1]

The phrase 'Heavenly Father' identifies God's relationship with his creatures. This is one of the most beautifully descriptive titles given to him. In the same manner God calls Jesus his 'Son'. 'This is my Son, whom I love; with him I am well pleased.'[2] Thus the Gospel *(Injil)* states that Jesus is the Son of God. He is called the Son of God by his disciples: 'You are the Christ (Messiah), the Son of the living God.'[3] Jesus himself confirmed this title. When the High Priest asked him, 'Are you the Christ, the Son of the Blessed One?' Jesus replied, 'I am. . . .'[4]

Objections

Some may say the terms 'Son of God' and 'Father' give one the idea of a physical relationship, and so should not be used. For Christians it would not be wise to abandon such terms since they have Jesus' full approval. We all know that 'fatherhood' and 'sonship' are used in various ways. For example, Muhammad Ali Jinnah is called the father of the Pakistani nation (Baba -e- Mellat), and Mahatma Gandhi is called the father of the Indian nation. In the Qur'an a wayfarer is called, 'Ibnu 'sabil' – son of the road.[5] This does not mean that the road has a wife or Jinnah and Gandhi were the physical fathers of their nations.

There are many similar examples. The city of Mecca is called '*Om-ul-Qura*' – the mother of villages.

Muhammad's cousin Ali was called '*Abu Turab*' – the father of dust. Even today it is quite common for elderly men and women to call any young person 'daughter' or 'son', even though they are not their real fathers and mothers. Therefore just as it is not necessary to force an offensive interpretation on the above examples, we should not force an offensive interpretation on the biblical statements about Jesus being the Son of God.

The heart of the matter

In the light of both the Qur'an and the Bible, if God can see and hear without having eyes and ears like ours, and if he can have a face and hands different from ours, and can sit on a throne different from ours, then it is also possible for him to have a Son in a different way from us.

Jesus as the Son of God

When the angel gave the glad tidings to Mary, he said, '. . . the holy one to be born will be called the Son of God'.[6] The Bible does not say that Jesus was called the Son of God just because he was born of Mary. Nor does it attempt to make a mere man into God or create a god beside the one true God. God alone is God.

The first & the last

The Bible states that Jesus is God's Word. 'In the beginning was the Word, and the Word was with God, and the Word was God. He was with God in the beginning.'[7] This passage tells us that Jesus is the eternal Word of God. As God is eternal, so also is Jesus his Son eternal. No one else has been called the Word of God other than Jesus. It was this eternal Word of God which almost two thousand years ago came from heaven into this world. He became man by being born of the virgin Mary.

Muslim friends do accept that God's eternal Word became a book. Why should it not be possible then, to accept that God's Word became a man, Jesus? Even the Qur'an, 600 years later, acknowledged that Jesus is the Word of God.[8]

The unique Sonship

It is often said that the expression 'son of God' is found in the Bible in the general context of humans being called children of God and, therefore, when Jesus claimed to be the Son of God he was merely speaking in a metaphorical sense.[9]

However, it is impossible to draw this conclusion from Jesus' statements about himself. He was not using this title in the same way as others who are called 'sons of God'. What more systematic, categorical and emphatic statement could there be than the following?

'All things have been committed to me by my Father. No-one knows who the Son is except the Father, and no-one knows who the Father is except the Son and those to whom the Son chooses to reveal him.'[10]

No other prophet, no other apostle used such language to identify himself. No wonder the Jews once testified, 'no-one ever spoke the way this man does'.[11]

He who has seen me

Jesus claimed that he had come from heaven to earth and that he had always existed.[12] He said, 'Before Abraham was born, I am!'[13] We may wonder what Jesus was claiming to be, but the people around him understood. Some of them picked up stones to stone him to death for blasphemy. These Jewish listeners had realized that Jesus claimed to have been alive before Abraham was born and that he was using the personal name of Yahweh, revealed to Moses ('I am', see Exodus 7:14), thus making himself equal with God.

Jesus prayed to God, 'Father, glorify me in your presence with the glory I had with you before the world began.'[14] He also told others, 'Anyone who has seen me has seen the Father.'[15]

Are these claims the same as saying that God has a partner? What was Jesus claiming? The plain answer is that Jesus was claiming to be of the same essence as God. He is the best possible representation of God. Jesus also said, '. . . the Father judges no-one, but has entrusted all judgement to the Son, that all may honour the Son just as they honour the Father, . . . who sent him'.[16]

Eye-witnesses of his majesty

At the transfiguration God told the disciples, 'This (Jesus) is my Son, whom I love; with him I am well pleased. Listen to him!'[17] Referring to this event, one of the apostles said, 'We did not follow cleverly invented stories when we told you about the power and coming of our Lord Jesus Christ, but we were eye-witnesses of his majesty. . . . We ourselves heard this voice that came from heaven when we were with him on the sacred mountain.'[18]

The crucial question

Why did God send his eternal Word to earth? Simply because he loves his creation and wanted to bring it back to himself. That is why the Bible says, 'Whoever believes in him may have eternal life.' Why? Because Jesus is the only way to reach the presence of God. Jesus said, 'I am the Way, the Truth, and the Life; no-one comes to the Father except through me.'[19] We are told that, 'Salvation is found in no-one else, for there is no other name under heaven given to men by which we must be saved.'[20]

References

1. Matthew 6:9–13
2. Matthew 3:17
3. Matthew 16:16
4. Mark 14:61,62
5. Qur'an 2:177; 4:171
6. Luke 1:34-35
7. John 1:1–2
8. Qur'an 3:45
9. Ahmad Deedat, *Christ in Islam*, pp. 28–29
10. Luke 10:22
11. John 7:46
12. John 6:51
13. John 8:58–59
14. John 17:5,24

15. John 14:9–10
16. John 5:22–23
17. Matthew 17:5
18. 2 Peter 1:16,18
19 John 14:6
20. Acts 4:12

Chapter 15

Jesus, the Great Teacher (Parables)

Although the teaching ministry of Christ lasted only three and a half years, during that time he showed that he was the world's master teacher. He performed great miracles and taught a new way of life. His teaching was simple. He used words the common people could understand, and took his illustrations from the things with which his listeners were familiar. Many of his principles were set forth in parables. A parable is a true-to-life story with a special meaning. In this chapter we examine a few of them.

The things Jesus taught are more important than his methods. He gave us a complete way of life, which he summed up in one sentence, 'So in everything, do to others what you would have them do to you, for this sums up the Law and the Prophets.'[1]

God's kingdom

One of the great themes of his teaching was God's kingdom. His claim was, 'The time has come. The kingdom of God is near. Repent and believe the good news.'[2]

This is a reminder to all of us that the world is not out of control. God is still in charge, but he has given us free-will. We are not like machines wound-up by God. Rather we are free, and yet ruled by a King, and that is God. When Jesus spoke of the kingdom of God it was to invite people to submit themselves to it. Jesus told parables to illustrate what he meant by God's kingdom.

The parable of the sower

'A farmer went out to sow his seed. As he was scattering the seed, some fell along the path, and the birds came and ate it up. Some fell on rocky places, where it did not have much soil. It sprang up quickly, because the soil was shallow. But when the sun came up, the plants were scorched, and they withered because they had no root. Other seed fell among thorns, which grew up and choked the plants. Still other seed fell on good soil, where it produced a crop – a hundred, sixty or thirty times what was sown.'[3]

Obviously the resulting crop depended on the kind of ground that the seed fell into. What Jesus meant here is that if our hearts are hard, bitter, and filled with pride and self sufficiency, then even if the good seed comes to us, even if we hear and learn about his kingdom, we won't accept it. However, if we accept

God's will in our lives, the kingdom of God will be within us.

A hidden treasure

On another occasion Jesus told of a treasure hidden in a field. A merchant found it '. . . and then in his joy went and sold all he had and bought the field.'[4] It is true that when we find the kingdom of God, we receive much joy, but there is a price to be paid. Our becoming a member of the kingdom of God, and following Jesus may offend many people. Our honesty may well make some people around us uncomfortable. We may lose friends, brothers and sisters. Our families may well turn against us. Joining this kingdom of God may mean the loss of a job, imprisonment, or even death. Jesus recognizes that you may have to pay a high price to come into this kingdom but it is still well-worth-while.

Once some of the Jewish leaders from the sect of the Pharisees asked Jesus when the kingdom of God would come.[5] Jesus replied, 'The kingdom of God does not come visibly, nor will people say, "Here it is" or "There it is" because the kingdom of God is in you.' Many people who were listening to Jesus were longing for a political revolution. They wanted Jesus to be their Messiah in a political sense, to overthrow the Roman rulers and release Palestine from its bondage. Jesus refused such a demand because that was not the real problem. Mankind's fundamental problem is not political. It is sin. Jesus came to deal with sin.[6] According to him, God's kingdom was a universal kingdom, not restricted to any particular people. Therefore he told them that this kingdom is within men's hearts. It was not something that was going to be established in the future, but something that was being established there and then. One can become a member of this kingdom by following Jesus and his commandments.

The greedy farmer

The ground of a certain rich man produced a good crop. He thought to himself, 'What shall I do? I have no place to store my crops.'

Then he said, 'This is what I'll do. I will tear down my barns and build bigger ones, and there I will store all my grain and my goods. And I'll say to myself, "You have plenty of good things laid up for many years. Take life easy; eat, drink and be merry." '

But God said to him, 'You fool! This very night your life will be demanded from you. Then who will get what you have prepared for yourself?'

This is how it will be with anyone who stores up things for himself but is not rich towards God. But seek his kingdom, and these things will be given to you as well.

(Luke 12:16–21;31)

The parable of the lost son

There was a man who had two sons. The younger one said to his father, 'Father, give me my share of the estate.' So he divided his property between them.

Not long after that, the younger son got together all he had, set off for a distant country and there squandered his wealth in wild living.

After he had spent everything, there was a severe famine in that whole country, and he began to be in need. So he went and hired himself out to a citizen of that country, who sent him to his fields to feed pigs. He longed to fill his stomach with the pods that the pigs were eating, but no-one gave him anything.

When he came to his senses, he said, 'How many of my father's hired men have food to spare, and here I am starving to death! I will set out and go back to my father and say to him: Father, I have sinned against heaven and against you. I am no longer worthy to be called your son; make me like one of your hired men.' So he got up and went to his father.

But while he was still a long way off, his father saw him and was filled with compassion for him; he ran to his son, threw his arms around him and kissed him.

The son said to him, 'Father, I have sinned heaven against heaven and against you. I am no longer worthy to be called your son.' But the father said to his servants, 'Quick! Bring the best robe and put it on him. Put a ring on his finger and sandals on his feet. Bring the fattened calf and kill it. Let's have a feast and celebrate. For this son of mine was dead and is alive again; he was lost and is found.' So they began to celebrate.

Meanwhile, the older son was in the field. When he came near the house, he heard music and dancing. So he called one of the servants and asked him what was going on. 'Your brother has come,' he replied, 'and your father has killed the fattened calf because he has him back safe and sound.'

The older brother became angry and refused to go in. So his father went out and pleaded with him. But he answered his father, 'Look! All these years I've been slaving for you and never disobeyed your orders. Yet you never gave me even a young goat so I could celebrate with my friends. But when this son of yours who has squandered your property with prostitutes comes home, you kill the fattened calf for him!'

'My son,' the father said, 'you are always with me, and everything I have is yours. But we had to celebrate and be glad, because this brother of yours was dead and is alive again; he was lost and is found.'

(Luke 15:11–32)

Jesus did not tell this parable just to entertain the people who were around him. He intended to show that God receives even the most wicked person who repents and turns to him, because he wants everyone to be saved and come to him through Jesus. In this parable we see how one may turn away from God to find his own way of adventure and folly. However God in his mercy and kindness awaits and leaves the door flung open for him expecting that one day this child of Adam may see a shaft of light and return to him.

Why Jesus?

Why should submission to Jesus be the only way to inherit the kingdom of God? It is because *he is the king of the kingdom*. He did not act like worldly rulers. He introduced a totally different concept of leadership. He advised his disciples: 'Whoever wants to become great among you must be your servant, and whoever wants to be first must be slave of all. For even the Son of Man did not come to be served, but to serve, and to give his life as a ransom for many.'[7] He demonstrated this concept by washing the feet of his disciples.[8] Later he gave his life for them and for us. On the other hand he did prove his authority and trustworthiness by the many signs he provided, and by the many prophecies he fulfilled particularly by getting out of the tomb. [Romans 1:4; cf. Romans 10:9]

Jesus gave his followers assurance about the future. At the day of judgement he will say to those who have chosen to follow his way, 'Come, you who are blessed by my Father; take your inheritance, the kingdom prepared for you since the creation of the world.'[9]

References

1. Matthew 7:12
2. Mark 1:14–15
3. Matthew 13:3–8
4. Matthew 13:44
5. Luke 17:20–21
6. John 6:15
7. Mark 10:43–45
8. John 13:4–17
9. Matthew 25:34

Chapter 16

Jesus: the Great Teacher (Miracles)

As we have learnt earlier, Jesus is not just a prophet. He is much more than that. The Bible declares him to be the King of Kings and Lord of Lords.[1] The things he did and said are witnesses to his authority and power. He said to some unbelieving Jews: 'Do not believe me unless I do what my Father does. But if I do it, even though you do not believe me, believe the miracles, that you may know and understand that the Father is in me, and I in the Father.'[2]

Both the Qur'an and the Bible agree that Jesus did miracles. He gave sight to the blind, and he raised the dead to life among other things. In the Gospels we find that through his sayings and miracles Jesus wanted to show the significance of his coming from God. He performed miracles in response to particular needs. It was never merely to prove that he could perform miracles, but because he had something more to teach people.

The first miracle

At a wedding party Jesus changed water into wine (see Glossary). It had such a beautiful taste that the guests had never tasted anything like it before.[3] Now what was Jesus showing by this? He was showing that he was bringing in something, [his kingdom], that was far better than anything that had gone before. We learn from this miracle that God is the Master of quality. Whoever and whatever we may be when we accept Jesus as our Saviour, he changes us, melts us, and moulds us into something of great quality.

Life to a child

A bewildered father came to Jesus and asked him if he would go back with him to the village where his child lay dying. Jesus said to the man, 'You may go. Your son will live.'[4] The father went back, and while he was still on the way, his servant met him and told him that the boy was living. He asked as to the time when his son got better and realized that it was the exact time at which Jesus had said to him, 'Your son will live.' He and his household believed in Jesus.

We learn from this event that Jesus has the power to overcome distances. God is never far from us. Jesus said, '. . . surely I am with you always . . .'[5] No wonder he was named Jesus, which means the Lord saves. We should turn to him who has unlimited power.

A man at the pool

The pool of Bethesda was well known in first-century Jerusalem. Crowds of sick people used to gather around this pool everyday. There was a legend that when the water was stirred up, the first sick person into the water would be healed.[6]

One day Jesus went to visit the pool and saw a sick man lying there on his mat. For thirty-eight years he had been paralysed. Jesus said to him, 'Do you want to be healed?' Then he told him to get up and pick up his mat and walk. The man was immediately cured and did what Jesus had told him.

What do we learn from this event? We may be the worst and most wretched person, but the door of repentance is open to us. Jesus can forgive and heal us, but it depends on our willingness. God's plan of salvation through Jesus cannot be forced on anyone. There has to be openness to God, to allow him to make us whole people. He is in control of the situation, but he will never force his way into our lives unless we are willing to accept Jesus as our saviour.

Feeding several thousand people

On one occasion Jesus amazed a crowd of over 5,000 by feeding them all, using just a few loaves of bread and some fish. Many people had gathered around him. The place was very remote and it was late in the day. The apostles wanted to send the people away, but Jesus wanted to feed them. One of the apostles found a boy who had five small barley loaves and two small fish. He asked Jesus, 'How far will they go among so many?'

But Jesus did not answer. Instead he directed his disciples to make all the people sit down in groups on the grass. Taking the five loaves and the two fish, he gave thanks, and broke the loaves. Then he gave them to his disciples to set before the people. They ate, and afterwards they collected twelve baskets full of broken pieces of bread and fish that were left.[7]

What do we learn?

People were looking for a Messiah who would look after them. They were more concerned about their bodily needs. They ran after Jesus to make him their king, but later Jesus told them clearly that his real purpose in coming to the world was to save people.[8] He told them that their forefathers had been given food and had been helped in their physical needs in the wilderness, but those people had not lived long. By contrast, the food Jesus brought lasts forever, and it is he himself on whom we have to feed.

For those who have believed in Jesus there is something more to be learned from this event. Here was a boy with only a few loaves and fish, but God was able to multiply them. Here is an encouragement for us; whatever we can give God of time, energy, and income, he is able to multiply the result. He is the Master of quantity.

Jesus walks on water

After feeding the multitude, Jesus asked his disciples to take a boat and go ahead of him. They left, and rowed towards their destination, but because of a strong wind blowing against them they were very slow. It was already dark and Jesus had not yet joined them. After they had rowed about three miles, they saw Jesus approaching the boat, walking on the water. He was about to pass by them, but when they saw him, they thought he was a ghost and cried out. Immediately he said to them, 'Take courage . . . Don't be afraid.'

When Peter saw this, he asked if he also would be able to walk on the water. Jesus said, 'Come.' Peter got down and walked on the water towards Jesus, but when he saw the wind, he was afraid and began to sink. Immediately Jesus reached out his hand and saved him.[9]

A lesson for us

Jesus is the Master of nature. When we decide to follow him, he says, 'Come and follow me.' And when we face trouble and cry to him to save us, he is there to help. He calmed a storm and enabled Peter to walk on the surface of the water. This may not seem very relevant to us today. However it teaches us that in every situation of life Jesus is present and his confidence and calmness are available to those who believe in him. Today Jesus also stills the storms in the hearts of many people. No matter what trouble, pain or sorrow there may be in a believer's life, with Jesus there is peace.

Jesus, the Master of life

Jesus gave sight to the blind, made the deaf to hear, and gave life to the dead. Lazarus had been dead for three days and had been buried, but when Jesus cried out at his tomb, 'Lazarus, come out', he came out alive.[10]

Thus, Jesus has the power to raise the dead. No wonder he said, 'I am the resurrection and the life. He who believes in me will live, even though he dies.'[11] Jesus is coming again to judge the world. He has promised to raise his followers to eternal life.[12]

Conclusion

The miracles and teaching of Jesus are, 'written that you may believe that Jesus is the Christ, the Son of God, and that by believing you may have life in his name.'[13]

References

1. Revelation 19:11–16
2. John 10:37–38
3. John 2:1–11
4. John 4:46–54
5. Matthew 28:20; cf. 1:22–24
6. John 5:1–9
7. John 6:1–14
8. John 6:22–71
9. John 6:16–21; Mark 6:47–50; Matthew 14:22–32
10. John 11: 1–45
11. John 11:25
12. John 6:40
13. John 20:31

Chapter 17

Jesus, the Great Teacher
(Faith & Action)

From the very beginning of his teaching, Jesus was a threat to the religious authorities, but many ordinary people followed him. These people were confused by the different ways in which their teachers interpreted the Torah. Their teachings were mostly about rituals and outward formality. However, Jesus came with a teaching which was radically different.

The Sabbath

The Sabbath is the seventh day of the week; a day that the Jews kept especially holy. The principle of a day of rest is very sound, but the Jews added all kinds of prohibitions, forbidding many activities taking place on the Sabbath. By doing so they missed its real meaning.

Jesus told people that on the Sabbath all good work must continue. For example, he deliberately healed people on that day. On one such Sabbath he stood up among the people and challenged them: 'Which is lawful on the Sabbath: to do good or to do evil, to save life or to kill?'[1] He then healed a man right in front of them all, and some Jewish leaders were so offended that they started to plan to kill him.[2] But Jesus did not stop doing good because of this. As we considered in the last chapter it was also on a Sabbath that Jesus healed the paralysed man at the pool of Bethesda.[3] As a result of this the leaders made further threats to Jesus' life.[4]

Jesus wanted to teach people two things. Firstly, that God has compassion for them every day of the week. Secondly, that people should not set up religious regulations, which come merely from men and not from God. We may laugh at the people of Jesus' days who followed man-made rituals and regulations, but we also have to ask ourselves whether the things we do are pleasing to God or not.

Prayer

Jesus taught a lot about prayer. He said that if we pray only in public, so that people may see how religious and pious we are, this is hypocrisy. God is not interested in such prayers. He said, 'When you pray, do not be like the hypocrites, for they love to pray standing in the synagogues and on the street corners to be seen by men . . .'[5]

His instructions were that worship of God should be in spirit and truth.[6] If our mind and heart are not right,

all our prayers are useless. He said that we should not
repeat things over and over again while praying.[7] The
Jews had many set prayers which they would simply
repeat at high speed. Jesus taught that such prayers are
of no benefit. God does not hear us just because we
use many words, or repeat the same words many times
in our prayers. He said, 'Learn from me.'[8]

How to pray?

He gave an example of prayer, which is sometimes
called the Lord's prayer.[9] However it would be more
appropriate to call John 17: 1–26 'the Lord's prayer'.

Jesus did not intend his disciples to repeat this
prayer verbatum. Rather he was giving them an idea
of what true prayer should be like. When praying we
would do well to ask God that his rule should be
effective here on this earth; to plead for our physical
and spiritual needs to be met; to appeal for forgiveness
and finally to acknowledge his sovereignty.

> *Our Father in heaven,*
> *hallowed be your name,*
> *your kingdom come,*
> *your will be done on earth as it is in heaven.*
> *Give us today our daily bread.*
> *Forgive us our debts,*
> *as we also have forgiven our debtors.*
> *And lead us not into temptation, but deliver us from the*
>   *evil one,*
> *for yours is the kingdom and the power and the glory for*
>   *ever.*
> *Amen.*

Jesus did not instruct us to pray facing Jerusalem or in any other direction. Nor did he give instructions about the movements of our bodies during our prayers. According to Jesus, God is more interested in the motives of our hearts.

One may ask, 'How much do I need to be in prayer?' Jesus spent long periods of time in prayer, both before important events and as a regular practice. The apostles did the same and advised other Christians to do so.

Prayer changes things. However, the Bible does not only tell us to have faith, but also that we are to put our faith into action. Prayer must not be regarded as a labour-saving device; God will not do for us the things that we can do for ourselves. He will listen to our prayers, and will help us in our difficulties. He will accept our prayers for the things that are best for us.

When Christians pray to God, they do so in the name of Jesus, because this is what Jesus commanded them to do. God first approached us in Jesus. Jesus himself said, 'My Father will give you whatever you ask in my name. Until now you have not asked for anything in my name. Ask and you will receive, and your joy will be complete.'[10]

Fasting

The question is often asked: 'Why do you Christians not fast?' Christians do fast,[11] but they do not fast during Ramadhan. Jesus said, 'When you fast, do not look sombre as the hypocrites do, for they disfigure their faces to show men they are fasting. I tell you the truth, they have received their reward in full. But when you fast, put oil on your head and wash your face, so that it will not be obvious to men that you are fasting, but only to your Father, who is unseen; and your Father, who sees what is done in secret, will reward you.'[12]

According to Jesus, fasting, like personal prayer, is something private, and should be carried out just between the individual believer and God. Jesus' emphasis was always on inner motivation, not outward appearance. People may pray and fast but still lack forgiveness. In the Bible a man named Cornelius is mentioned. He was a God-fearing person who had a good reputation among friends and foe alike. He fasted and prayed, yet lacked forgiveness. Because of his sincerity though, God sent Peter, an apostle of Christ to talk to him, so that he would find forgiveness. Peter spoke to him about Christ: his perfect life, his sufferings, and his death on the cross. He told him about Jesus' resurrection and his return as Judge. It was not until Cornelius believed in Jesus that he found forgiveness.[13]

Is not this the kind of fasting I have chosen: to loose the chains of injustice and untie the cords of the yoke, to set the oppressed free and break every yoke?

Is is not to share your food with the hungry and to provide the poor wanderer with shelter – when you see the naked, to clothe him, and not turn away from your own flesh and blood?   (Isaiah 58:6–7)

Giving

The Pharisees of Jesus' day were very concerned about giving to God exactly one tenth of all their income, even down to a tiny quantity of herbs such as mint. In fact they were neglecting what was really important by making a big show of their giving to God. Jesus said, 'Be careful not to do your "acts of righteousness" before men, to be seen by them. If you do, you will have no reward from your Father in heaven. So when you give to the needy, do not announce it with trumpets, as the hypocrites do in the synagogues and on the streets, to be honoured by men. I tell you the truth, they have received their reward in full. But when you give to the needy, do not let your left hand know what your right hand is doing, so that your giving may be in secret. Then your Father, who sees what is done in secret, will reward you.'[14]

To show that one should be helpful, without expecting any reward from people, Jesus told the story of the Good Samaritan. This story is a great example of generous love for others.

The good Samaritan

Jesus said: 'A man was going down from Jerusalem to Jericho, when he fell into the hands of robbers. They stripped him of his clothes, beat him and went away, leaving him half-dead.

'A priest happened to be going down the same road, and when he saw the man, he passed by on the other side. So too, a Levite, when he came to the place and saw him, passed by on the other side. But a Samaritan, as he

travelled, came where the man was; and when he saw
him, he took pity on him. He went to him and bandaged
his wounds, pouring on oil and wine. Then he put the
man on his own donkey, brought him to an inn and took
care of him. The next day he took out two silver coins
and gave them to the innkeeper. "Look after him", he
said, "and when I return, I will reimburse you for any
extra expense you may have."

'Which of these three do you think was a neighbour
to the man who fell into the hands of robbers?' The expert
in the law replied, 'The one who had mercy on him.' Jesus
told him, 'Go and do likewise.'   (Luke 10: 30–37)

Many people today talk about the need for good
relations between people of different backgrounds and
ethnic origins. Long ago, Jesus gave this one principle:
'Love your neighbour as yourself.'[15] Not only are the
people next door my neighbours, but so is the stranger
who travels with me for a short while on the bus or
train. This generous love is supremely shown in Jesus'
life, by the giving of himself to save mankind.[16] Let us
follow his footsteps in love and truth.

References

1. Mark 3:4
2. Mark 3:6–6
3. John 5:1–15
4. John 5:16–18
5. Matthew 6:5–6
6. John 4:24
7. Matthew 6:7
8. Matthew 11:29

9. Matthew 6:9–13
10. John 16:23–24
11. Matthew 17:21; 1 Corinthians 7:5; Acts 13:3
12. Matthew 6:16–18
13. Acts 10:1–48
14. Matthew 6:1–4
15. Luke 10:27
16. 2 Corinthians 8:9

Chapter 18

Jesus, the Great Sacrifice

I stood beside Ahmad watching his father sacrificing a lamb with a knife. It was the festival called *Eid al-Adha* and Muslims celebrate it every year. I wondered why Muslims sacrificed so many animals every year. That was several years ago when I did not know much about the meaning of the event. Very soon, like others, I came to know that it was in memory of when God tested Abraham by asking for the sacrifice of his son. Abraham obeyed, but at the right moment God provided a ram as a substitute for Abraham's son.

Adam & Eve

The Bible in fact tells us that sacrifice goes back before Abraham. When Adam was created, God warned him not to eat from the tree of knowledge, or he would surely die.[1] Adam and Eve disobeyed God. They realized they were naked, and felt ashamed, so they tried to cover themselves with leaves.[2] This story is also mentioned in the Qur'an.[3]

Cain & Abel

The first two sons of Adam and Eve were Cain and Abel.[4] The Bible shows that they had been taught to sacrifice to God. Abel acted accordingly and his offering was accepted, but Cain did not, and his offering was rejected. The Qur'an confirms that Cain's offering was not accepted.[5] When we look at this story in the context of the whole Bible we see that Adam's family had been taught a particular way to approach God. This was to offer sacrifice to him. Later, God showed that we deserve to die for our sin, and so a substitute is needed, a ransom, (*fidyah*).

Abraham & his son

This substitution is illustrated in the case of Abraham and his son. God told Abraham to offer up his son, and Abraham obeyed. When he lifted his knife to kill his son, God told him to stop and provided a ram instead. So the ram died in place of Abraham's son.[6]

The Passover lamb

Another remarkable example was the Passover lamb. The Israelites were in cruel bondage in Egypt. The ruler, Pharaoh, wouldn't let them go free to worship God. Therefore God sent Moses to deliver them. After sending many plagues to Egypt, God said he would kill all the firstborn children in that land. However, God also provided a substitute for the firstborn of Israel. Moses commanded his people to slaughter a lamb and sprinkle its blood on their door posts. The angel of God would then pass over every door which had the blood on it, and the firstborn in that house would be spared. God fulfilled his promise and the firstborn of Israel were saved.[7]

The law of Moses

In the law of Moses, in the book of Leviticus, God revealed that the way for mankind to approach him is through sacrifice.[8] Later he said, 'Without the shedding of blood there is no forgiveness.'[9] Moses explained the method of sacrifice to the Israelites. The sinner was to take a perfect animal to the door of the temple of God. There he was to put his hands on it, symbolically transferring his sins onto the animal. Next he had to kill it and the priest would sprinkle its blood at the foot of the altar, and offer the rest to God on the altar. God would accept the animal's death in place of the death of the sinner.[10]

A question

How can an animal die for a man, when a man is of much greater value than any animal? The animal did not take away man's sin, it was merely a symbol pointing to what was to come. God permitted such a situation until the perfect sacrifice would be offered for all sin. This offering would be for the sin of all the people who had ever lived or would live.

The great sacrifice

After Moses, many prophets of God came to prophesy about this great sacrifice. One such prophet was Isaiah. He made a very astonishing prophecy which was fulfilled centuries later in Jesus who accomplished God's purpose. [Read Isaiah 52:13–15; 53:1–12]

The testimony of John the Baptist

God sent John the Baptist, known as Hazrat Yahya, to be the last of these prophets. John was the forerunner of Jesus. He called people to repent and be baptized. One day when Jesus appeared on the shore of the Jordan river, John cried out, 'Look, the Lamb of God, who takes away the sin of the world! This is the one I meant when I said, "A man who comes after me has surpassed me because he was before me." '[11]

The testimony of Jesus

Jesus himself declared that he had come to give his life as a ransom for many[12] and that anyone who believed in him, would have eternal life.[13] He fulfilled his task by being crucified. On the cross he cried, 'It is finished', to tell mankind that God's purpose had been completed.[14] The long awaited promise to Abraham had been fulfilled. Jesus once said, 'Your father Abraham rejoiced at the thought of seeing my day; he saw it and was glad.'[15] The Qur'an said that God ransomed Abraham with a great sacrifice.[16] Can there be anything greater than Jesus' sacrifice of himself?

This is God's way and it is the only way. We see that on the third day Jesus rose victoriously from the dead to show that those who believed in him would enjoy eternal life with God. After his resurrection, Jesus said, 'This is what I told you while I was still with you: Everything must be fulfilled that is written about me in the Law of Moses, the Prophets and the Psalms . . . This is what is written: The Christ will suffer and rise from the dead on the third day, and repentance and forgiveness of sins will be preached in his name to all nations, beginning at Jerusalem.'[17]

God with us

Dear friend, God commanded Adam and Eve to leave his presence, not because he hated them, but because they had disobeyed. They had sinned. To bring them, and the whole of mankind, back into fellowship with him, he planned to rescue them. When the good news about Jesus was given, the prophet Isaiah said, '. . . they will call him Immanuel'[18] which means, 'God with us'.[19] Jesus spent only about 30–35 years on this earth but before his bodily ascension he said, '. . . Surely I am with you always, to the very end of the age.'[20]

Who would refuse this Saviour who offers us an assurance such as nobody else has ever given? Let us follow his teaching.

References

1. Genesis 2:17
2. Genesis 3:7,8
3. Qur'an 20:115–123

 4. Genesis 4:1–16;
 5. Qur'an 5:27–32
 6. Genesis 22:1–18; Qur'an 37:102–109
 7. Exodus 12
 8. Leviticus 17:1–12
 9. Hebrew 9:22.
10. Leviticus 4
11. John 1:29,30
12. Matthew 20:28
13. John 3:14–16
14. John 19:30
15. John 8:56
16. Qur'an 37:102–109
17. Luke 24:44,46,47
18. Isaiah 7:14.
19. Matthew 1:23.
20. Matthew 28:20

Chapter 19

The Second Coming of Jesus

Islam and Christianity share the belief that the same Jesus, who lived on this earth and was raised alive into heaven, will return to this world at the end of the age.

The return of Jesus in Islam

Popular Muslim traditions assert that when Jesus comes back, he will convert the world to Islam, destroy the antichrist, marry and have children. Later he will die and be buried next to Muhammad's grave in Medina.[1]

To support this doctrine, Muslims refer to the following verse in the Qur'an:

'And (Jesus) shall be a Sign (for the coming of) the Hour (of Judgement): Therefore have no doubt about the (Hour) but follow ye Me: this is a Straight way.' (A. Yusuf Ali, Surah 43:61).

The majority of Muslim commentators take this

verse to be a prophecy about the second coming of Jesus. This event is known as the '*Nuzul-i-Isa*' and also as the '*Nuzul-i-Masih*', the 'descent' of Jesus.

One of the Muslim traditions states: 'Abu Huraira reported that the Messenger of Allah (may peace be upon him) said: By Him in Whose hand is my life, the son of Mary (may peace be upon him) will soon descend among you as a just judge. He will break crosses, kill swine and abolish *jizya* (poll tax), and the wealth will pour forth to such an extent that no one will accept it.'[2]

Such are the references to the return of Jesus in Islam, but there are major differences between Christians and Muslims regarding his coming.

The return of Jesus in the Bible

Jesus' return is one of the great themes of the Bible. However, there is no suggestion that on his return Jesus will live as an ordinary human being, let alone that he will die and be buried. When Christians speak of Jesus' second coming from heaven, they obviously already believe in his first coming from heaven. Both beliefs go together and cannot be separated from each other.

On numerous occasions Jesus said that he had come down from heaven and that he would come again.[3] This second coming is to be different from the first. The Conquering King will come as Mighty Judge.

After witnessing Jesus' ascension, two angels told the disciples that he would come back from heaven in a similar manner as they had seen him go into heaven.[4]

Yet Jesus made it clear that his second coming would be a public event; as lightning comes from the east and flashes to the west, so will be his coming.[5] He warned us that there would be false prophets and false Messiahs, claiming to be the returned Christ. However, it will be easy for everyone to recognize his coming, because it will be witnessed throughout the whole world, by everyone, instantly.

The work upon his return

Jesus will send his angels to gather up all those who believe in him, and will take them to heaven.[6] There will be a resurrection of all those who have died. As Jesus said, 'For a time is coming when all who are in their graves will hear his voice and come out – those who have done good will rise to live, and those who have done evil will rise to be condemned.'[7]

Thus Jesus taught that his return is to be a climactic event. He will judge the living and the dead, rewarding those who love and obey him with eternal life and casting the rest into darkness to remain there forever.

The assurance that Christians have is that they will be raised to eternal life on that Day, not because they are worthy of it through their good deeds, but because of their faith in Jesus. Jesus said that on that day the righteous will shine like the sun.[8]

If God holds our deeds in a balance on that great day, then we will all stand condemned. However many good works we may have done, they will never be enough to bridge the gap which separates us from God. However, all this has been done for us in this life through Jesus. A believer in Christ's redemption does not do good deeds in order to earn a place in paradise. Rather, he does them because he loves Jesus. Jesus said, 'If you love me, you will obey what I command . . . I have set you an example that you should do as I have done for you.'[9] We praise God for the great gift of salvation; but for those who have never entered God's kingdom in this life there will be eternal condemnation. Jesus himself made this clear again and again.[10]

The time factor

Jesus said that he will return when people do not expect him. For example, he said that his coming will be like a thief in the night. 'If the owner of the house had known at what time of night the thief was coming, he would have kept watch and would not have let his house be broken into. So you also must be ready, because the Son of Man will come at an hour when you do not expect him.'[11]

Jesus also said that his coming will be like the flood which came in the time of Noah. People were eating and drinking and were carrying on their normal daily work right up to the day that Noah entered the ark and the flood came.[12]

Some may say that two thousand years have passed and yet he has still not come. The Bible teaches that God loves his creation, and he does not want anyone to perish, so he is patient. He wants everyone to repent and be saved.[13] But you can be sure, he is keeping his promise. One day, at his own appointed time he will be here. As each day passes by, we get nearer to his coming. Time in fact is running out. There may be no chance tomorrow.

Jesus alone has conquered death. He alone dwells in heavenly glory far above the billions of men and women on earth, both dead and living. It is he who alone will return, shining in all his heavenly majesty, to award the crown of life to all who love him and have remained faithful to him even unto death. Everyone should surrender to him and be saved by his grace.

The purpose of Jesus' return

To raise the dead

'Do not be amazed at this, for a time is coming when all who are in their graves will hear his voice and come out – those who have done good will rise to live, and those who have done evil will rise to be condemned.'[14]

To judge all men

'See, the Lord is coming with thousands upon thousands of his holy ones to judge everyone, and to convict all the ungodly of all the ungodly acts they have done in the ungodly way, and of all the harsh words ungodly sinners have spoken against him.'[15]

To reward the righteous and the unrighteous

'When the Son of Man comes in his glory, and all the angels with him, he will sit on his throne in heavenly glory. All the nations will be gathered before him, and he will separate the people one from another as a shepherd separates the sheep from the goats. He will put the sheep on his right and the goats on his left.

Then the King will say to those on his right, "Come, you who are blessed by my Father; take your inheritance, the kingdom prepared for you since the creation of the world . . ." Then he will say to those on his left, "Depart from me, you who are cursed, into the eternal fire prepared for the devil and his angels." '[16]

To deliver the kingdom to the Father

'Since death came through a man (Adam), the resurrection of the dead comes also through a man. For as in Adam all die, so in Christ all will be made alive. But each in his own turn: Christ, the firstfruits; then, when he comes, those who belong to him. Then the end will come, when he hands over the kingdom to God the Father after he has destroyed all dominion, authority and power. For he must reign until he has put all his enemies under his feet. The last enemy to be destroyed is death . . . When he has done this, then the Son himself will be made subject to him who put everything under him, so that God may be all in all.'[17]

References

1. Wali ad Din, *Mishkat Al Masabih*, tr. James Robson, (Lahore, 1980), Vol II. pp. 1159–1160.
2. *Sahih Muslim*, Vol.1, p.92
3. John 3:13; 8:23; 14:23; 16:28; Matthew 25:31,32; 26:64
4. Acts 1:10,11
5. Matthew 24:27; Revelation 1:7
6. Matthew 24:31
7. John 5:28,29

8. Matthew 13:43
9. John 13:15; 14:15;
10. John 3:18,36
11. Matthew 24:43–44
12. Matthew 24:37–39
13. 2 Peter 3:9
14. John 5:28,29
15. Jude 14–15
16. Matthew 25:31–34, 41
17. 1 Corinthians 15:21–26, 28

Chapter 20

Christ, our Life

Before the birth of Christ, many prophets and saints came to prepare the way for him. The Bible puts this message very clearly. 'In the past God spoke to our forefathers through the prophets at many times and in various ways, but in these last days he has spoken to us by his Son, whom he appointed heir of all things, and through whom he made the universe.'[1]

Jesus said, 'Come to me . . . and I will give you rest.'[2] Elsewhere, as we saw earlier, he claimed, 'I am the way and the truth and the life. No one comes to the Father except by me.'[3] Many have realized the truth of the above verse: that Jesus is indeed the only way to God and that eternal life is to be found only in him. Without him we would remain separated from God, hopelessly lost in eternal darkness.

Jesus once said to the Jews, 'You diligently study the Scriptures because you think that by them you possess eternal life. These are the Scriptures that testify about me.'[4] Just to study and gain knowledge is not enough. It is our response which matters.

What should I do then?

I believe in Jesus. I believe he is the Saviour of humanity. What must I do then to follow him and to enter the kingdom of God?

A Jewish ruler once said to Jesus, 'Rabbi, we know you are a teacher who has come from God. For no-one could perform the miraculous signs you are doing if God were not with him.'[5] In response Jesus said, 'I tell you the truth, no-one can see the kingdom of God unless he is born again.'[6] He added by way of further explanation: 'no-one can enter the kingdom of God unless he is born of water and the Spirit.'[7]

Before his ascension, Jesus gave his disciples the great commission, 'Go into all the world and preach the good news to all creation. Whoever believes and is baptized will be saved, but whoever does not believe will be condemned.'[8]

This is a very clear command and explains why, after Jesus' ascension, Peter preached to the Jews at the feast of Pentecost. He told them how Jesus' coming had been predicted in the Scriptures, and how he had been crucified and raised from the dead. Many understood the message and wanted to follow Jesus as their Saviour. Therefore they asked the apostles what they should do. Peter replied, 'Repent and be baptized, every one of you, in the name of Jesus Christ for the forgiveness of your sins. And you will receive the gift of the Holy Spirit.' The Bible says that those who accepted his message that day and were baptized, numbered about three thousand.[9]

What Peter said raises two questions:

1. Who is the Holy Spirit?
2. What is Baptism?

Who is the Holy Spirit?

We read about the Holy Spirit throughout the Bible, from the first chapter of Genesis to the last chapter of Revelation.[10] This shows us clearly that God's Spirit is everywhere. He is called by several names in the Bible:

The Spirit of God	(Genesis 1:2; Ephesians 4:30)
The Holy Spirit	(Acts 1:5,8; 2:1–4)
The Counsellor	(John 14:16)
The Spirit of truth	(John 14:17; 15:26)
The Spirit of Christ	(Romans 8:9)
The Spirit of his Son	(Galatians 4:6)
The Spirit of holiness	(Romans 1:4)
The Spirit of wisdom	(Ephesians 1:17)

The coming of the Holy Spirit

The Bible tells us that, although the Holy Spirit is at work everywhere, he specifically came on certain people in the Old Testament in order to enable them to do special tasks. Read for example: Exodus 31:3; 1 Samuel 10:6; 1 Chronicles 28:12; Isaiah 42:1; Ezekiel 11:5.

In the New Testament we see that Jesus promised that this Holy Spirit would come and live in every believer. This began on the day of Pentecost when the

Holy Spirit completely changed the disciples of Jesus. They became more courageous in preaching and teaching about their Saviour.

The work of the Holy Spirit today

It is through the message of the Bible that the Holy Spirit convicts people of their sinfulness.[11] The Holy Spirit equips us to serve God and others. The more we surrender ourselves to the guidance and control of the Holy Spirit, the more our lives become like Christ's. This is because the Holy Spirit produces 'love, joy, peace, patience, kindness, goodness, faithfulness, gentleness and self-control'.[12] By ourselves we are completely unable to live lives which demonstrate all these qualities. However, God's Holy Spirit makes it possible for our lives to be like this.

What is baptism

Almost all Greek scholars agree that the word baptize as used in the Scriptures means to dip, submerge, or immerse. The first person to baptize people in the New Testament was John the Baptist. In baptism we appeal to God for forgiveness.[13]

Philip & the Ethiopian

When the message of Jesus was accepted by someone seeking the truth, he was baptized. Philip, a disciple of Jesus, was guided by an angel to meet an Ethiopian. Philip talked to him about Jesus, from the book of the prophet Isaiah. The Ethiopian believed what Philip had said and asked for baptism. Philip baptized him there and then.[14]

What does baptism signify?

Baptism symbolizes dying and being buried with Jesus and then, just as Jesus rose, the believer is raised to a new life in Christ. As the Bible says, '. . . all of us who were baptized into Christ Jesus were baptized into his death . . . We were therefore buried with him through baptism into death in order that, just as Christ was raised from the dead . . . we too may live a new life.' We should count ourselves dead to sin. Our past sins having been forgiven we should not let sin control our lives.[15]

Living with Christ

Jesus said, 'Let your light shine before men, that they may see your good deeds and praise your Father in heaven.'[16] A believer in Christ is expected to reflect his love, joy and peace. If you follow Christ, some people will not mind your new faith but many others will be upset because you have given your life to him.

Jesus understands such situations and he has warned us that following him will not be easy. However, he also promised that he will give us peace in our hearts. He said, 'Do not be afraid of those who kill the body but cannot kill the soul. Rather, be afraid of the One who can destroy both soul and body in hell. Are not two sparrows sold for a penny? Yet not one of them will fall to the ground abandoned by your Father and apart from the will of your Father. And even the very hairs of your head are all numbered. So don't be afraid; you are worth more than many sparrows. Whoever acknowledges me before men, I will also acknowledge him before my Father in heaven.'[17]

A changed life

A Christian obeys God out of love, not out of fear. He serves him with joy and gladness. A Christian cannot live without Christ. Jesus said, 'Remain in me, and I will remain in you. No branch can bear fruit by itself; it must remain in the vine. Neither can you bear fruit unless you remain in me. I am the vine, you are the branches. If a man remains in me and I in him, he will bear much fruit; apart from me you can do nothing.'[18]

This reminds us that we cannot overcome Satan and his followers by ourselves. Only Jesus can, because he has defeated Satan once for all. Satan always tries to harm those who have accepted Christ and shake their faith. He stirs up opposition to try and make Jesus' followers deny their faith in him. True believers continue to listen to Jesus in such situations. He warns us of opposition but reassures us that he is all-powerful. 'All this I have told you so that you will not go astray. They will put you out of the synagogue; in fact, a time is coming when anyone who kills you will think he is offering a service to God. They will do such things because they have not known the Father or me . . . I have told you these things, so that in me you may have peace. In this world you will have trouble. But take heart! I have overcome the world.'[19]

References

1. Hebrews 1:1–2
2. Matthew 11:28
3. John 14:6
4. John 5:39
5. John 3:2
6. John 3:3
7. John 3:5
8. Mark 16:15–16
9. Acts 2:14–42
10. Genesis 1:2; Revelation 22:17
11. John 16:8–11
12. Galatians 5:22–23
13. John 3:23; Acts 22:16; 1 Peter 3:21
14. Acts 8:26–40
15. Romans 6:3–4, 11
16. Matthew 5:16
17. Matthew 10:28–32
18. John 15:4–5
19. John 16:1–3,33

Glossary

Abraham: who lived about 4,000 years ago, the ancestor of both the Arabs and the Jews. God made a covenant (special agreement) with Abraham that, if he remained faithful to God, he would have many descendants and the land of Canaan would be theirs for ever (Genesis 13:15-16). Furthermore, God promised Abraham that all people on earth would be blessed through him (Genesis 12:3). Abraham's biography is related in Genesis 11–25.

Acts: the fifth book of the New Testament. It gives a record of the early Christian Church after Jesus' resurrection. It was written by Luke.

Adam & Eve: the first man and woman created by God. Adam was created first and then Eve was created as a companion for him. They lived in the Garden of Eden, but after disobeying God, they were cast out of his presence. Their biography is related in Genesis 2 and 3.

Ahmadiyya: a sect of Islam, founded by Mirza Ghulam Ahmad (1835–1908), who declared himself to be a renewer of the Islamic faith.

Alexander the Great: a king of Macedonia and one of the greatest generals in history. He conquered much of the then civilized world and brought Greek culture to those places. He lived from 356 to 323 BC.

Apostles: (Envoys) usually the twelve men whom Jesus chose to be with him during his ministry on earth. They were: Andrew; Bartholomew; James, son of Zebedee; John; James, son of Alphaeus; Judas Iscariot; Thaddaeus; Matthew; Simon Peter; Philip; Simon the Zealot and Thomas. After Judas' death, Matthias took his place as an apostle.

Apostle: means 'one who is sent'. In Matthew chapter 10:5 Jesus calls the twelve that he personally sent out on a mission, 'apostles'. An apostle of Jesus had to have seen Jesus and to be a witness of his resurrection (Acts 1:22). The apostle Paul was personally commissioned by the Lord Jesus after his ascension. Acts 22:14,15, 1 Corinthians 9:1 and 15:8.

In Acts 14:4,14 Paul and Barnabas are also called apostles in a different sense. They had been 'sent' by the church at Antioch on a missionary journey. Acts 13:2,3 and 14:26,27. So they were in that sense, apostles of the church at Antioch. These two uses of the word apostle must not be confused.

Ascension: the dramatic departure of the risen Christ from earth to heaven, which took place forty days after the resurrection. The accounts of the ascension can be found in Acts 1:9–11; Mark 16:19; Luke 24:50–51.

Autograph: an original manuscript in the author's handwriting.

Bethlehem: a small town in Jordan, 5 miles south of Jerusalem. It was the birth place of Jesus as prophesied in Micah 5:2.

Circumcise: circumcision was the physical sign of God's original covenant with his people (Genesis 17:10–11).

Codex: a forerunner of the modern book. It was made by folding several sheets of papyrus in the middle and sewing them together along the fold. A codex was written on both sides.

Covenant: a binding contract made by one party and accepted by another.

Crucifixion: the most severe method of torture and execution used by the Romans and many other nations of the ancient world. It was used for slaves and criminals. The victim was nailed to a wooden stake or gibbet and left to die.

Daniel: a prophet who lived around 600 BC The Old Testament book named after him deals with historical events in Babylon and shows Daniel's faith in God. It also includes visions of future events.

Dead Sea Scrolls: the oldest known manuscripts of any books of the Bible. They contain all the books of the Old Testament, except Esther. A few of these books are almost complete. They were found in the 1940s and 1950s in caves near the north-west shores of the Dead Sea. Now they are kept in the 'Shrine of the Book', part of the Israel Museum in Jerusalem.

Ezekiel: a priest and prophet who lived around 600 BC and stressed the importance of following God's law. There is an Old Testament book named after him which contains the following prophecies:

    chapters *1–24:* prophecies of how God would punish the people of Judah for their sins.

    chapters *25–32:* prophecies against neighbouring countries for defying God's will and rejoicing over the misfortunes of the Israelites.

    chapters *33–48:* prophecies of Israel's restoration and salvation.

Forgiveness: means the removing of our sin due to God's graciousness. This is all made possible through Christ (Ephesians 1:7). Read also Exodus 34:6–7 and Psalm 103:10–12. The New Testament makes it clear that the forgiven sinner must forgive others.

Furqan: a standard or reference against which everything must be judged.

Gospel: literally means 'good information'.

Immanuel: means 'God with us'. One of the names given to Jesus.

Isaiah: a prophet who lived about 700 BC. In the Old Testament book which bears his name, there are prophecies foretelling Jesus' coming.

Jeremiah: a prophet who lived around 600 BC There is a book in the Old Testament named after him in which Jeremiah tried to reform the life of the Jews and spoke of the individual's relationship with God. He also warned of the Babylonian invasion.

Job: is the central figure of the Old Testament book which bears his name. This book is the story of Job's suffering, the lessons God taught him from it and his ultimate salvation.

John the Baptist (Hazrat Yahya): a great prophet who lived from about 7 BC to 28 AD. He was a forerunner of Jesus and prepared the way for him. He urged people to repent of their sins and baptized them in the River Jordan.

John: one of the twelve apostles and brother of James, son of Zebedee. He was inspired by God to write the fourth Gospel and the three letters bearing his name.

Jonah: the book in the Old Testament named after him tells how God called Jonah to prophesy to the people of Nineveh. It was written about 400 BC.

Josephus: a Jewish historian who wrote a 20-volume history of the Jews from their beginning to the end of Nero's reign. He was the governor of Galilee when war broke out between the Jews and the Romans in 66 AD.

Judas Iscariot: the apostle who betrayed Jesus. He was the treasurer of the apostles.

Kingdom of God: the spiritual reign of God. The term 'kingdom of God', or 'kingdom of Heaven', refers to God's rule of grace where evil is overcome. Those who live in this kingdom know righteousness, happiness, peace and joy (cf. Romans 14:17).

Letters: the 21 books of the New Testament from Romans to Jude, also known as 'Epistles'. They were formal and instructive, many being written by the apostle Paul to the Christian congregations he founded.

Manuscript: a hand-written record, from before the invention of printing, which can often be identified with a certain period of history by the material on which it is written and the style of writing.

Masoretic text: the basic text of the Old Testament, used for centuries in schools and synagogues. It was produced by the Masoretes, a school of rabbis in Palestine and Babylonia in the eighth and ninth centuries AD who were the preservers of the Old Testament writings.

Micah: a prophet who lived in the late 700s BC and whose name means 'who is like the Lord'. There is a book in the Old Testament which bears his name. Through him God spoke about people being more concerned with ceremonies than with true godliness; about oppression of the poor; about true and false prophets and about the Messiah coming from Bethlehem.

Miracles: mighty acts of God that cannot be explained through the known laws of nature.

Nazareth: a quite insignificant town in northern Israel, in the Roman province of Galilee. It was the home of Jesus during his early years.

Nebuchadnezzar: the King of Babylon from 605-562 BC. Nebuchadnezzar set up many building projects and, under his rule, Babylon became one of the world's most magnificent cities. He also captured and destroyed Jerusalem.

Nineveh: the last capital of the ancient Assyrian Empire, situated on the east bank of the River Tigris. In 612 BC it was captured and destroyed and was not discovered by archaeologists until the 1800s.

Passover: the Jewish festival which celebrates the Israelites' flight from slavery in Egypt in about 1200 BC (Exodus 12). The Passover celebrations are held in March or April each year.

Peter: a leading apostle of Jesus. His original name was Simon but Jesus gave him the name Peter, meaning 'rock'. He was a leader of the early Christian community.

Philo: a leader of the Jewish community in the early part of the first century AD. He wrote on philosophical and theological subjects.

Pilate: the Roman governor at the time of Jesus' crucifixion. He governed Judea from 26–36 AD. Jesus was put on trial before Pilate who wanted to release him, but was afraid of losing his office.

Revelation: the last book of the New Testament, revealed to the apostle John. It contains messages to the churches and visions of the future, depicting the end of the present age. Its Greek title means 'unveiling' or 'disclosure' of the hidden things known only to God.

Ruth: the name of an Old Testament book which tells the story of Ruth, a Moabite woman who married an Israelite. After the death of her husband, Ruth devoted herself to her mother-in-law and became a follower of Israel's God. She was an ancestor of the Lord Jesus.

Sabbath: (Hebrew, rest) the seventh day of the week from sunset Friday to sunset Saturday. God completed the creation of the universe in six days. He required the Israelites to set the seventh day of every week apart for worship and rest, Deuteronomy 5:12–15. This 'rest' was also figurative of the eternal rest awaiting the faithful after death, Hebrews 4:8–11.

Christians are not required to observe the Jewish Sabbaths, Colossians 2:16. They are required to meet together and remember the Lord's death, burial and resurrection. This is done by sharing a cup of wine or grape juice representing his shed blood and an unleavened loaf representing his body, Matthew 26:26–30, Mark 14:22–25; and 1 Corinthians 11:20–26. The first day of the week (which approximates our Sunday) was set apart for this, Acts 20:7. It is the day upon which Jesus rose from the dead. This weekly observance was known as 'the breaking of the bread' and 'the Lord's Supper', Acts 2:42, 20:7 and 1 Corinthians 11:20.

Sacrifice: the offering of the blood or flesh of an animal to God in gratitude or payment for sin. By offering an animal to God, the Hebrew people were giving another life in place of their own. God demanded that they offer him the best, a young unblemished male animal.

Septuagint: the oldest Greek translation of the Old Testament. It is believed that an Egyptian king had seventy Jewish scholars translate the Torah for the benefit of Greek-speaking Jews. This translation began around 250 BC. The most famous manuscripts of the Septuagint are the Vaticanus, the Alexandrinus and the Sinaiticus.

Simon of Cyrene: the man from the area called Cyrene who was forced to carry Jesus' cross (Matthew 27:32; Mark 15:21: Luke 23:26).

Sin: deviation from the law or will of God, 'missing the mark'. Sin is rebellion against God and because God is holy, he cannot tolerate sin. However, God himself has provided in Jesus the solution to this problem of sin. Read Romans 3:23; 6:23 and 1 John 3:4.

Surah: Written also as *Sura*, means a row or series, chapter of the Qur'an.

Tacitus: a historian who lived from 55–120 AD. He described Roman history from Augustus to Nero.

Tahrif: means 'corruption', alteration. It refers to the charge made by Muslim theologians against Christians of having modified and falsified the Gospel.

Testament: similar meaning to covenant. In Arabic it is *Misaq* or *Ahd*.

Wine: In the Bible wine is not necessarily fermented/alcoholic. It can refer to grape juice still in the grapes and to freshly pressed grape juice.

Zechariah: a prophet who lived about 520 BC and wrote the book in the Old Testament bearing his name. He urged the people of Jerusalem to rebuild the temple and prophesied about God's victory over evil and the coming Messiah.